100 Buildings 100 Years

100 Buildings 100 Years

The Twentieth Century Society

BATSFORD

First published in the United Kingdom in 2014 by Batsford

1 Gower Street

London WC1E 6HD

An imprint of Pavilion Books Group

Volume copyright © Batsford, 2014

Text © C20 Society, 2014

Pictures © see page 207

ISBN: 9781849941938

10 9 8 7 6 5 4 3 2 1

Reproduction by Rival Colour Ltd, UK

Printed by 1010 Printing International Ltd, China

This book can be ordered direct from the publisher at the website:
www.pavilionbooks.com or try your local bookshop.

C20 Society:

Editorial advisory panel: Timothy Brittain-Catlin, Catherine Croft,

Elain Harwood, Alan Powers, Peter Ruback

Editor: Susannah Charlton, with Elain Harwood

Picture researcher: Jennie Walmsley

Permissions: Penny Laughton

Batsford:

Project editor: Lucy Smith

Designer: Zoë Anspach

Find out more about the C20 Society and join at www.c20society.org.uk

Front cover De La Warr Pavilion
(see page 60).

Page 2 Post Office (BT) Tower
(see page 107).

Contents

The Twentieth Century Society

What we do and why we have compiled 100 Buildings.

This selection of 100 buildings has been put together by the C20 Society, from nominations made by our members and supporters, to mark the centenary of the period under our remit – buildings completed from 1914 onwards. There are plenty of buildings here that are really well known, but quite a few that aren't. The purpose of the selection was not to nominate the 'best' or the 'most representative' building constructed in each year (that would be a very tricky and specious task) but to gather together some favourites, and show a diverse group that would demonstrate just how fantastic and varied the architecture of the last 100 years has been. Inevitably lots have been left out. My particular regrets include no Camden housing, and no Bill

Mitchell sculptures. Some of the selected buildings are ones that would not exist today if the C20 Society had not campaigned to save them; a few, alas, have been demolished already. Together they make the most compelling argument possible for the ongoing necessity of the C20 Society's work. There is still much work to be done to ensure the long-term survival of the best architecture and design of our period and, while the popularity of some of these examples is now well established, the merits of many remain contentious.

Many conservation groups focused on twentieth century architecture are very partisan – that is, they look exclusively at one style or type of building. For instance, there are many Art Deco societies, most

Opposite Interior of Farnley Hey by Peter Womersley (see page 95).

Above Alexandra Road Estate, 1972–8, by Camden Architect's Department.

Above A detail of a cast concrete sculpture by William Mitchell, University of Salford, 1966.

notably in the US – in Miami and Los Angeles, cities which were extensively developed in the 1920s and 1930s – and in Napier, New Zealand, which was rebuilt after an earthquake in 1931. DoCoMoMo, which has 59 chapters in countries as far apart as Scotland and Taiwan, is exclusively interested in the architectural heritage of the Modern Movement – essentially functionalist architecture born of the machine age.

In contrast, the C20 Society has always been interested in all twentieth century buildings, regardless of the style they followed (including those which claimed to have no style, but be the pure product of objective problem solving). As you will see, some in this selection were heavily influenced by what was being constructed abroad and extensively photographed and published in the architectural press here. Others draw only on British precedents, and could not have been designed anywhere else. We are aware that our own tastes have changed, as our knowledge has grown. There is no one person's selection here; not everyone agrees all of the time.

Our former Chairman Gavin Stamp still regrets the loss of Sir Edwin Cooper's Lloyd's building (see page 27), and is not a fan of the Richard Rogers replacement, now widely regarded as a high tech masterpiece and listed at Grade I – at the request of the C20 Society. We are still all talking to one another.

The Society regularly researches buildings and proposes them for listing. Recommendations are passed to English Heritage, but the final decision maker is a politician, in the Department of Culture Media and Sport – we've challenged the objectivity of several holders of the post. By law, we are consulted by every local authority planning department in England every time a building owner makes an application for permission to demolish or substantially change a listed building.

My first major case as Director of the C20 Society was Greenside (see page 63), a classic listed Modern Movement house, demolished by its owner who didn't like it, and was not convinced it could be successfully refurbished. I had assumed that this type of house, now iconic and already recognised as a very rare example of pioneering design from a key period of innovation, would not be at major risk. However, it proved very vulnerable because it was a relatively small and dilapidated property, on quite a large plot, in a prestigious and unique location beside Wentworth Golf Course.

A larger new house on the site would have been worth many millions. Although the owner was convicted of unlawful demolition (a sentence which gave him a criminal record), for the C20 Society it was a frustrating demonstration of the weakness of our heritage protection system. The fine imposed was far less than the profit the owner looked set to make from rebuilding. Although we were subsequently successful in arguing that no new building could be erected, as the site had been returned to being a vacant plot in the green belt, the building was still gone forever. It made me realise that the Society had to concentrate not just on

winning legal battles, but on doing our best to get as many people as possible to share our enthusiasm, and see the potential for keeping and continuing to use and enjoy twentieth century buildings.

To that end we regularly run visits and tours, including trips to many of the buildings featured in this book. We have organised conferences to further academic research, and published books and magazines on lots of previously largely unrecognised architects and little-known buildings. Right now we are still trying to explain that Brutalist buildings aren't meant to be brutal, and that although postmodernism may be out of fashion, the best examples will come to be appreciated again in due course, if they manage to survive. We are also filling in the gaps with the architecture of earlier decades, searching out examples that are perhaps less flashy or obvious than some of their contemporaries – the ones that weren't published in the magazines

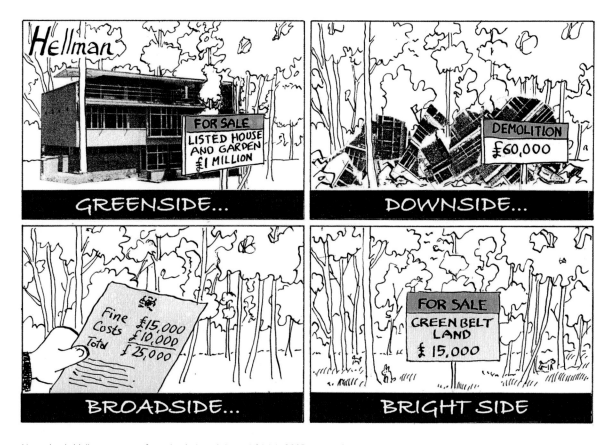

Above Louis Hellman cartoon from the *Architect's Journal*, 21 July 2005, on the fate of Greenside.

Above Louis Hellman Southbank cartoon from the *Architects' Journal*, 11 July 2013, of opponents to the South Bank's proposed extensions.

when they were new, and were less accessible to the dominant media hub of London.

We know that one reason people feel wary of taking on twentieth century buildings is that they are not sure how to set about repairing them, or how to sensitively upgrade them to meet modern expectations. We know that underfloor heating has frequently failed and that, while single glazing may have been a reasonable choice when electricity was cheap and plentiful and no one had heard of global warming, it is hard to live with now. Friends still giggle when I tell them I'm off to teach my annual course on the Conservation of Historic Concrete, but it is not an oxymoron, nor is 'concrete cancer' an insurmountable problem (in my view it is a confusing misnomer, often paired with 'concrete monstrosity' – both are phrases designed to induce panic and loathing). Most concrete buildings are very robust, and can be repaired much as stone buildings can. Concrete can age and weather beautifully, developing a patina – though I accept that it doesn't always manage it. The myth that many of us wanted to believe, that buildings could be made from materials that would need no maintenance, was just that: a myth. Looking back at what architects were actually saying, it's hard to work out where the myth actually came from – many were scrupulous about specifying the necessity for simple housekeeping (clearing gutters, painting windows),

which we know are equally essential with buildings of earlier periods. And of course, some elements of building fabric have needed replacing, but then what's the fundamental difference between relaying an asphalt roof and re-thatching a cottage?

Some twentieth century buildings required enormous amounts of traditional craft skills. In some cases this is very apparent, but in others the care which went into working out details is forgotten; top quality concrete relies on very good carpentry skills to make formwork, and many buildings which have a factory aesthetic are in fact bespoke. Having said that, if factory-made elements are used, there is no good reason why we should consider them fundamentally less worth saving than hand-crafted ones. Much can be learnt about the world at any date from the materials used in the buildings erected then, whether facts about transport and trade links, the availability or lack of labour, or the priorities of one function over another.

Much of this evidence can be lost in overly drastic makeovers. While buildings of earlier centuries are generally 'restored to their former splendour', with much effort made to keep as much historic fabric as possible and research and replicate materials, twentieth century buildings are often totally reinvented. At times this is a sensible thing to do, but some schemes go too far and, although billed as conservation projects, they actually preserve little of what made the original structure special in the first

Above The Bear Ravine, Dudley Zoo, by Lubetkin and Tecton, 1937.

Above The Commonwealth Institute, 1962, by RMJM (Grade II*) before the site was radically developed as housing and the Design Museum.

place. The recent redevelopment of Park Hill flats in Sheffield is a classic example of this. Images of the site once it had been stripped out show just how much went in the skip. Now a kind of fetishistic false history has been created in the flats by exposing the bare concrete frame, once clothed with modest timber architraves and plaster finishes. The Design Museum's move to the old Commonwealth Institute building in Kensington raises similar issues. Again, little more than a skeleton has been kept: just the structural components of the hyperbolic paraboloid roof remain. What will be the long-term verdict on what's been termed architect John Pawson's twenty-first century 'rebirth' of a building that arguably did not need major surgery? The C20 Society would have preferred a solution that was more compatible with the original concept of a building whose interior provided a particularly mesmerising experience.

These buildings don't need melodramatic make-overs – they don't need the equivalent of false eyelashes, a fake tan and six-inch heels. They need a little gentle tidying up, new services and sympathetic owners who will take pleasure and pride in them. Unlike classic cars, classic architecture can't stay in the garage until it is sunny outside and everything is freshly polished. While an unfashionable work of art can be relegated to the basement store to be appreciated again at a future date, a demolished building cannot be rebuilt. The C20 Society exists to ensure good examples do survive, even when commercial pressure and market forces might favour redevelopment. This is a book of photographs but I hope it is a book at that will make readers want to go and see buildings for real. Architecture impacts on all the senses, and is part of all our lives. The best twentieth century buildings enrich us all.

Catherine Croft
Director, C20 Society
www.c20society.org.uk

100 Years Timeline

Social and Political History and International Landmarks	Year	UK Architecture and Planning
First World War begins	1914	C20 Society remit begins
	1916–20	Experiments with new materials and techniques, like prefabrication and Crittall windows, prompted by inflation having pushed up the cost of building materials
First World War ends	1918	
	1919	Housing (or Addison) Act promises 'Homes for Heroes'
Empire Exhibition, Wembley	1924	Erection of temporary Cenotaph in Whitehall (see page 34); Royal Fine Art Commission created to look into questions of public amenity or artistic importance; Mechanical vibration of concrete
L'Exposition Internationale des Arts Décoratifs et Industriels Modernes in Paris – title gives us the term Art Deco, popularised by Bevis Hillier in the late 1960s	1925	New Ways, Northampton, by Peter Behrens for W.J. Bassett-Loake is the first Modern Movement house in Britain
General Strike	1926	
	1927	Vers une Architecture by Le Corbusier published in English as Towards a New Architecture
The first 'talkies' seen in Britain; Decline and Fall by Evelyn Waugh published	1928	Big new super cinemas start to be built
Wall Street Crash	1929	High and Over, Amersham, the first truly modern house in the UK
Stockholm Exhibition – a model for the Festival of Britain	1930	
Empire State Building, New York	1931	Charles Holden's Sudbury Town is the first modern London Underground station
		Royal Corinthian Yacht Club, Burnham-on-Crouch, by Joseph Emberton
	1932	Hoover Factory, Great West Road (see Firestone Factory page 46); Boots D10 factory opens (see page 52)
Hitler comes to power in Germany; Jewish emigration starts; Unemployment in the UK rose to 2.5 million	1933	

1934 — Penguin Pool, London Zoo, by Lubetkin and Tecton and Lawn Road Flats (see page 58)

The Modern House by F.R.S.Yorke published

1935 — Highpoint One by Lubetkin and Tecton; De La Warr Pavilion (see page 60)

1936 — Crystal Palace burns down

Jarrow March; Constitutional crisis as Edward VII abdicates the throne in order to marry Mrs Simpson

1937 — Walter Gropius and Marcel Breuer leave for USA as little work in UK

1938 — Pillar to Post by Osbert Lancaster published (see page 28)

Glasgow Empire Exhibition

1939 — 1–3 Willow Road, Hampstead, by Ernő Goldfinger

Second World War declared 3 September

1940–1 — Introduction of building licences imposes controls on raw materials (to 1954)

1942

First Mies van der Rohe skyscrapers in Chicago

Beveridge report on a social security system to challenge the five giants of 'Want, Disease, Ignorance, Squalor and Idleness'

1943 — Exhibitions on Swedish and American housing propose prefab housing

1944 — Fine Building by Maxwell Fry published

Town and Country Planning Act enables local authorities to compulsorily acquire sites for redevelopment and introduces the listing of historic buildings

6 June: Normandy Landings: 'D-Day'

Education Act makes all schooling free and establishes the 11 plus, and grammar, secondary modern and technical schools

1945

Second Word War ends; Labour, under Clement Attlee, wins the General Election with its first ever majority

1946 — Programme to build housing, schools and factories to cope with bomb damage and baby boom

Powell and Moya win competition for Churchill Gardens flats in Pimlico, London

New Towns Act: Stevenage the first New Town – 13 more follow by 1950; Hertfordshire programme of prefabricated schools begins

Timeline 1947–1956

Above the timeline (architectural events):

- **1947** — New controls on building introduced by Stafford Cripps; Restrictions on private house building rigorously enforced; Town and Country Planning Act, the major post-war legislation covering redevelopment, compensation, green belts and the listing of buildings
- Frederick Gibberd appointed architect of Harlow
- **1948** — Royal Festival Hall commissioned as centrepiece for the Festival of Britain
- First national Code of Practice for reinforced concrete in the UK (CP114)
- **1950** — Rebuilding of bombed cities, notably Plymouth (see page 79) and Coventry begins
- Frederick Gibberd wins limited competition for Heathrow airport
- **1951** — Festival of Britain takes place
- The first of Pevsner's *Buildings of England* series is published
- Gibberd's The Lawn, in Harlow, is Britain's first ten-storey 'point' block
- **1952** — Golden Lane housing competition for the City of London won by Geoffry Powell of Chamberlin, Powell and Bon
- Town Development Act encourages the expansion of towns like Swindon
- **1953** — Changes in housing policy encourage slum clearance, putting pressure on city centres
- **1954** — End of building licensing in November
- Opening of the LCC's first large comprehensive school at Kidbrooke, London
- **1955** — Reyner Banham's essay 'The New Brutalism' published in the *Architectural Review*
- **1956** — LCC eases restrictions on tall buildings in London
- Span's first scheme Parkleys (Richmond borders) opens, a landmark in low-cost housing

Below the timeline (general events):

- **1947** — Coal shortages, electricity failures and a run on the pound
- Nationalisation of coal industry (Act of 1946)
- **1948** — Start of National Health Service in May
- Nationalisation of electricity industry
- Equitable Savings and Loan Association in Portland, Oregon is the first curtain-wall building
- **1950** — Iron and steel nationalised by second Labour government
- **1951** — Mies van der Rohe's Farnsworth House in Falls River, near Chicago
- Conservatives return to power; they encourage more, yet cheaper, schools and housing
- **1952** — Queen Elizabeth II accedes to the throne on the death of George VI
- London's last trams run; iron and steel denationalised
- **1953** — The Coronation causes a demand for television sets
- **1955** — ITV launched, and the film *Rock around the Clock* promotes new youth culture
- **1956** — *Waiting for Godot* opens in Britain, *Look Back in Anger* is premiered
- The Suez Crisis delays several building projects

Start of Vietnam War (1956–75)

This is Tomorrow exhibition

White Paper on technical education creates Colleges of Advanced Technology

Macmillan becomes Prime Minister, and says Britons 'have never had it so good'

1957 Housing Act controls rents and evictions after Rachman scandal. Many large landowners prefer to sell up to local authorities for redevelopment

Nottinghamshire County Council opens its first prefabricated (CLASP) school, designed to ride subsidence caused by mining

The first publicly funded theatre opens in Coventry

Sussex University College founded, the first of a programme of new universities around the country

Shelagh Delaney's A Taste of Honey first performed

1958 Arne Jacobsen appointed architect for St Catherine's College, Oxford; Competition for Churchill College, Cambridge launched

Preston Bypass, Britain's first stretch of motorway, opened

M1 opens from Watford to Crick

1959 Schemes for tall towers include Millbank Tower, Centre Point and the Economist Group

Penguin Books found not guilty of obscenity in the Lady Chatterley's Lover trial

1960 St Paul's Bow Common by Maguire and Murray is first centrally-planned post-war church

The first birth-control pill

Opening of Keeling House, London and Park Hill, Sheffield: high-density flats on slum clearance sites

New universities approved for York and Norwich; Chamberlin, Powell and Bon masterplan for Leeds University

The Beatles perform for the first time at the Cavern Club, Liverpool

1961 First proposals for the Brunswick Centre by Leslie Martin and Patrick Hodgkinson, as a medium-rise, mixed-use development, after tall towers are rejected (see page 182)

John Darbourne, aged 23, wins competition for Lillington Gardens in Pimlico with a medium-rise brick scheme

Boom in building means shortages of building material and labour, and government encourages prefabrication

Cuban missile crisis

1962 Basil Spence's Coventry Cathedral opens, with Britten's 'War Requiem'

Centre Point by Richard Seifert and Partners, and Millbank Tower by Ronald Ward and Partners completed, dramatically changing London's skyline

Completion of Leicester University Engineering Tower by Stirling and Gowan (started 1959)

Buchanan report, *Traffic in Towns*, is a best-seller: it recommends the organisation of towns into precincts separated by improved roads, and the segregation of pedestrians and vehicles.

Ministry of Housing and Local Government looks at low-rise, high-density housing with scheme at West Ham

George Brown imposes a ban on new office buildings in London

Opening of the Economist Building in London by Alison and Peter Smithson

Washington, Redditch and Runcorn declared new towns

GLC develop Thamesmead as a quasi-new town

Team 4 (Georgie Wolton, Wendy Cheesman, Norman Foster and Richard Rogers, with Su Rogers) build Reliance Controls, Swindon, a light steel-framed factory

Opening of the Severn Bridge

Conservation areas introduced; End of a system whereby a listing has to be confirmed by a listed building in order to prevent demolition

Designation of Milton Keynes as a new town, and expansion of Northampton and Peterborough

Gas explosion at Ronan Point, Newham, causes collapse with four deaths. It promts a reaction against tall housing blocks and prefabrication generally

Ralph Erskine appointed to rebuild Newcastle's Byker neighbourhood

1962

1963

1964

1965

1966

1967

1968

1969

Hard winter delays building and increases unemployment

Profumo scandal; John F. Kennedy assassinated 22 November

Robbins Report on technical education, recommending the widening of higher education and provision of more courses in applied science and technology

Labour win narrow election victory; Harold Wilson goverment elected on a modernisation agenda

South East regional plan estimates another 1,250,000 people will need to be housed over the next 20 years, and proposes three new cities in the region

Reform of London government creates Greater London Council (GLC) and fewer, larger London boroughs

Labour re-elected with larger majority

Complexity and Contradition in Architecture by Robert Venturi published

Government launches 'I'm Backing Britain' campaign amid concerns over weakening of the pound

BBC launches colour television for Wimbledon

Riots in Paris; student occupations at London School of Economics and Hornsey School of Art

Pound devalued

1970	Norman Foster builds a lightweight office building of steel and glass for IBM in Cosham	Conservatives returned to power with Edward Heath as Prime Minister
1971	Richard Rogers and Renzo Piano win competition for the Pompidou Centre in Paris	Decimalisation amid rising inflation
1972	Town and Country Planning Act consolidates previous planning and conservation legislation; First Modern Movement buildings listed (Pevsner 50)	Demolition of Pruitt-Igoe housing project in St Louis, Missouri, begins
1973		Oil crisis
1974	Creation of the Public Service Architects section within Department of Environment; Many authorities rush to commission new buildings rather than see their reserves pass to the new authority	Return of Labour Government amid miner's strike; Reform of Local Authorities outside London
1975	'A Tonic to the Nation' exhibition about the Festival of Britain at the V&A	Reform of the British economy driven by the International Monetary Fund
1977		Elizabeth II's Silver Jubilee
1978	Richard Rogers commissioned to design Lloyd's Building	Winter of Discontent
1979	Thirties Society, forerunner of the Twentieth Century Society, founded; Thirties exhibition at the Hayward Gallery, London	Conservatives elected on 3 May and Margaret Thatcher becomes first woman Prime Minister; End of public housing programme in November
1980	Demolition of the Art Deco Firestone Factory, the Society's first prominent case	
1981	150 inter-war buildings proposed for listing, prompted by the loss of the Firestone Factory; Lutyens exhibition at the Hayward Gallery, London	Rupert Murdoch buys *The Times*; Prince of Wales marries Lady Diana Spencer; Riots in Brixton, south London and Liverpool
1982		Falklands War (2 April–14 June)

Timeline

1983 — National Heritage Act creates English Heritage

1984 — The Prince of Wales calls the proposed extension to the National Gallery a 'monstrous carbuncle' in a speech at a dinner marking the 150th anniversary of the RIBA

Privatisation of British Telecom; followed by coal, railways and nuclear energy

1985–6 — Society campaign to save Sir George Gilbert Scott's iconic red telephone boxes

'Big Bang' deregulation of the financial markets leads to relocation of banks outside the city

1986 — 'New Architecture: Foster Rogers Stirling' exhibition at the Royal Academy

1987 — Bracken House becomes first post-war listed building (see page 100)

Lord Elton introduces the 30-year rule and ten-year rule for post-war listing

1988 — Economist Group Building the first to be listed under the ten-year rule

1989 — Berlin Wall comes down, symbolising the end of the Cold War

1990 — Planning (Listed Buildings and Conservation Areas) Act

1991 — One Canada Square by I.M. Pei among the first buildings completed at Canary Wharf, on the Isle of Dogs

English Heritage Post-War Listing Steering Group set up, chaired by Bridget Cherry

Willis Faber Dumas listed, the first post-war building to have management guidelines

1992 — Thirties Society changes its name to the Twentieth Century Society

Black Wednesday: the pound crashes out of the European Exchange rate mechanism

1994 — Waterloo International station by Grimshaw Architects welcomes the first Eurostar

1996 — Public consultation on candidates for post-war listing: *Something Worth Keeping?*

RIBA Stirling Prize inaugurated with a £20,000 purse, named after James Stirling who died in 1992

1997 — Tony Blair leads New Labour to a landslide victory

1999 — Commision for Architecture and the Built Environment founded

Richard Rogers publishes Urban Task Force report encouraging good design in cities and development on brownfield sites

Modern Britain 1929–39 exhibition at the Design Museum

Keeling House by Lasdun sold by Tower Hamlets to a private developer

2000 — Millennium Dome designed by Richard Rogers hosts an exhibition to celebrate the start of the Third Millennium

Tate Modern opens in Gilbert Scott's Bankside Power Station, converted by Herzog and de Meuron

2001 — Brynmawr rubber factory in Wales demolished

New York's iconic Twin Towers at the World Trade Center are attacked by terrorists on 11 September

2003 — Greenside, a Grade II-listed modernist house by Connell, Ward and Lucas, demolished without consent

Start of the Iraq War (2003–11)

2004 — Demolition of the Tricorn Centre in Portsmouth begins

2005 — C20 Society becomes statutory consultee for applications for listed building consent involving demolition of listed buildings, putting it on the same footing as other amenity societies like SPAB and the Victorian Society

2007 — Frink's Desert Quartet sculptures listed at Grade II* and become the youngest listing

Eurostar moves to St Pancras International after extensive renovation of the Grade I listed station and hotel

Sub-prime mortgage crisis in the USA triggers recession

2008 — Housing and Regeneration Act

2010 — Demolition of Gateshead's Trinity Square car park, featured in film *Get Carter*

Conservatives form coalition with Liberal Democrats after hung election result

2011 — Lloyd's Building listed Grade I; English Heritage's National Heritage Protection Plan launches

2012 — Olympics held in London

2013 — Preston Bus Station listed Grade II

1914

King Edward VII Galleries, British Museum

Architect: Sir John Burnet
Location: Great Russell Street, London
Type: Museum
Listed Grade I

On 7th May 1914, attended by ambassadors from the principal European countries that would be at war with each other three months later, King George V opened the major extension to the British Museum, for which his father had laid the foundation stone in 1907. The completed section (only part of an ambitious plan to rebuild all three undeveloped sides of the Museum's island site) represented the height of achievement in modern classicism, bringing a knighthood to its Paris-trained Glaswegian designer.

Burnet was a highly creative experimental designer, yet possessed of a sense of the appropriate for each occasion. The drama lies within the cool Ionic exterior, in the complex staircase with its gilded lift cage and re-invented classical orders. This building looks two ways – back to the Greek Revival of 100 years before, and forwards to steel framed structures and the poetic classicism of Josef Plecnik and E. Gunnar Asplund.

Alan Powers

1915 · Well Hall Estate

Architect: Frank Baines
Location: Eltham, Greater London
Type: Housing

In 1915, increased munitions production became crucial. The workforce at Woolwich Arsenal was more than doubled and a site at Eltham selected for 1,298 dwellings, completed by the end of the year to designs by a team led by Frank Baines, chief architect of the Office of Works.

They believed that the estate should look 'as if it had grown and not merely been dropped there', and with a deliberately picturesque sequence of unfolding street scenes, composed largely of terraces, with a mixture of wall and roof materials, arranged along the contours, the estate avoided the rigidity of a military encampment that might easily have been the outcome. Ironically, the many jettied gables facing the streets led it to be described as the 'German village', and its relatively high cost was influential in determining a plainer character for later developments. The estate has been a conservation area since 1971, with an Article 4 Direction, controlling external features like windows, since 1978.

Alan Powers

1916 Holland House

Architect: H P Berlage
Location: 1–4 Bury Street, London
Type: Commercial/offices
Listed Grade II

I find it hard to believe that Holland House was built during the First World War (although the Netherlands were neutral). Designed for Dutch shipping company Muller by Berlage, the eminent Dutch architect, it seems to me to mark the transition from Art Nouveau to Art Deco and introduces something continental and exciting to London's cityscape.

A steel-framed building, its green glazed walls rising from a black plinth cleverly appear solid when viewed from certain angles. The windows only become apparent as you move to face the building head on from the open space around the Gherkin.

On one corner, a stylised relief of a ship steaming forward seems to symbolise the role of shipping companies at the time being in the forefront of design and style, much like this building. Holland House is unexpected, innovative and intriguing. It makes me want to book a sea crossing to Europe!

Sarah Wittekind

1917

Cardington Airship Hangars

Engineers: A J Main and Co. of Glasgow
Location: Former RAF Cardington, Bedfordshire
Type: Transport
Listed Grade II*

No.1 Shed is a vast steel structure built on farmland used by the Royal Flying Corps. It was used to construct airships, but the first – the R31 – was commissioned only five days before the Armistice.

In 1926–8 the shed was extended to 812 feet and joined by a second hangar, re-erected from Pulham, Norfolk, and similarly extended. The flat surrounding countryside only enhanced their dramatic scale seen from afar. A programme of civil airships commissioned by Ramsay MacDonald ended when the R101 crashed in October 1930, but the buildings survived as bases for barrage balloons in the Second World War.

The RAF sold the site in 1999–2000. Housing was built on the surrounding land, but the hangars have been restored and No.1 Shed is again being used to construct airships, this time filled with helium. It is Europe's only airship hangar from the First World War to survive *in situ*.

Elain Harwood

1918 St Andrew's Church of Scotland

Architect: Courtenay Melville Crickmer, under the supervision of Raymond Unwin
Location: Loanwath Road, Gretna, Dumfries and Galloway
Type: Place of worship
Listed Grade B

The Great War demanded increasing supplies of munitions. Dangerous cordite had to be manufactured (using nitroglycerine) somewhere safely remote, yet near good railways. Gretna and Eastriggs on the Solway were developed rapidly: a factory 9 miles long, with 20,000 workers, mainly women. Housing, shops and a cinema were provided, and churches for the main denominations – Episcopal, Roman Catholic and Presbyterian. Unwin, co-architect of Letchworth, was in overall charge: he appointed a Garden City colleague, C.M. Crickmer, as resident architect.

Rough cast over brick with an Italianate tower, it 'is very simply designed as a war building, depending for its effect on a broad dignified treatment.' (*Annandale Observer*).

St Andrew was used by both Church of Scotland and United Free congregations. All Saints Episcopal (probably Geoffry Lucas, 1917), St Ninian's RC, now Anvil Hall wedding venue (C. Evelyn Simmons, 1918) and St John Eastriggs (Unwin, 1917) also survive, but there is barely a trace of the factory.

Alec Hamilton

The Inter-war Decades
Gavin Stamp

The catalyst for the foundation in 1979 of what was at first called the Thirties Society was the proposal to demolish the home of Lloyd's of London in the City, a magnificent classical building designed by Sir Edwin Cooper in the 1920s. There was then a feeling, shared by several historians and others, that the architecture of the inter-war decades was insufficiently appreciated and that it was coming under threat, so that a new preservation society was needed to take up the cause where the scope of the Victorian Society ended. For architecture did not stop in the fateful year 1914 (any more than it was once officially deemed to do in 1714) and the Gothic Revival and Arts and Crafts Movement continued after the Great War – if, arguably, with a little less vigour. What also carried on was the monumental classicism of the Edwardian years, now disciplined and refined by older architects like Cooper.

In 1979 there was, in fact, statutory protection in place for a handful of buildings erected in the period 1914–39. In 1970 50 inter-war buildings had been listed by the Ministry of Housing & Local Government. Most, but by no means all, were the works of the pioneering architects of the Modern Movement, notably Maxwell Fry, Wells Coates, Connell, Ward and Lucas, Joseph Emberton, Berthold Lubetkin and Ernő Goldfinger, but significant works by Clough Williams-Ellis and H.S. Goodhart-Rendel were also included as well as a number of London Underground stations by Charles Holden. Over the following decade, other inter-war buildings were added to the list, including some remarkable cinemas and several works by Cooper. The Lloyd's building itself, indeed, was in fact listed, but that was not enough to save it once both the architectural establishment and the City of London supported its replacement.

Above The Post Office, Cranbrook, Kent, with K6 telephone boxes.

The problem at the time – and since – was a prevailing prejudice against 20th century classical, or traditional, buildings. It is unfair to blame Nikolaus Pevsner for the belief that architecture is somehow deviant if it is not 'of our time', but the fact is that many architects, particularly those who had been young in the 1930s and were committed to the Modern Movement, regarded buildings like Lloyds as irrelevant and reactionary, while the many modernistic or Art Deco buildings of the period were dismissed as meretricious, vulgar and worthless. And such attitudes had become conventional. There had been a 'Battle of the Styles' in the 1930s which, as Sir Giles Gilbert Scott noted in his Presidential Address to the Royal Institute of British Architects (RIBA) in 1933, echoed that of the 1850s between classic and Gothic. He himself sought compromise – 'I hold

Above 55 Broadway, London, by Charles Holden, built 1927–9.

'Pseudish' (his clever name for a version of Spanish Colonial) and 'Modernistic' in addition to 'Twentieth-Century Functional'.

As in the Edwardian decade, the classical tradition remained very strong during both inter-war decades, although there were many and diverse variations on the theme. Architects who had made their names before 1914, and even in the later Victorian years – Cooper, Reginald Blomfield, Herbert Baker (who cleverly fused the classic with the vernacular in Winchester and Oxford), Curtis Green and the incomparable Edwin Lutyens – carried on and secured large commissions. Lutyens, above all, was interested in developing the tradition, playing subtle games and abstracting its forms which he did, above all, in his war memorials – a building type which, for melancholy reasons, was very important right through the 1920s. Younger classical architects such as Albert Richardson became interested in the Regency for the lessons it provided for making the classical language relevant and modern.

Others, notably Grey Wornum, the competition-winning architect of the new headquarters of the RIBA, looked to Sweden, to 'Swedish Grace', for ways of modernising classical precedents. Continental European architecture, indeed, had a strong influence on British architecture after the mid-1920s, as did modern American classicism, as can be seen in Herbert Rowse's accomplished commercial blocks in Liverpool.

Classicism was almost compulsory for government and administrative buildings. Most new town halls were grand statements, usually with a portico, and a remarkable number were designed by E. Vincent Harris who, adept as a planner, was a serial competition winner. Sometimes the columns in those porticoes were fully developed Corinthian, but towards the end of the period they were more likely to be simple square piers. 'Stripped classicism' was ubiquitous by 1939, and was the essence of Holden's much admired new stations for the London Underground. Osbert Lancaster categorised this manner politically, as either 'Third Empire' or 'Marxist Non-Aryan' (that is, either Nazi or Stalinist), but in truth it was an international style which can also be seen as the architecture of

no brief either for the extreme diehard traditionalist or the extreme modernist and it seems to me idle to compare styles and say that one is better than another.' Many of his contemporaries agreed. British architecture in the period 1914–39 was characterised by compromise as well as by experiment, and there was no one prevailing or dominant style.

From the outset, therefore, the Thirties Society was committed to defending good architecture in any and all styles: classical as well as modern, the moderne or Art Deco and even the greatly despised Tudor. And, in surveying the period and seeking representative buildings, it is important to take seriously works, not only in the principal historical styles, but also in all the inflexions so wittily and brilliantly categorised (and satirised) by Osbert Lancaster in his two essential cartoon histories of architecture published in 1938 and 1939, *Pillar to Post* and *Homes Sweet Homes*: 'Bankers' Georgian', 'Curzon Street Baroque', 'Vogue Regency', 'Stockbrokers' Tudor' and its variants ('Wimbledon Transitional', 'Aldwych Farcical', 'By-Pass Variegated'), 'Park Lane...' and 'LCC Residential' (almost identical),

Above The interior of Lloyd's of London by Sir Edwin Cooper, 1925–8.

democracy, whether in New Deal America or in such large buildings as Walthamstow or Dagenham town halls.

Classicism was not always grand. In England, if not in Scotland, neo-georgian was the most common expression of the tradition. It was a style which could be seen as a reticent, gentlemanly manner of building rooted in tradition but also providing a basis for a universal modern architecture. It was thoroughly appropriate for domestic architecture, both houses and blocks of flats – in Welwyn Garden City it was fused with the Arts and Crafts – and schools, and also for the many Post Offices and telephone

exchanges designed by the Office of Works, which remain such tactful and dignified contributions to the urban scene and which deserve greater respect than they often receive.

If classicism carried on, so did the Gothic. Many accomplished church architects – Edward Maufe, Harold Gibbons and above all the great Giles Gilbert Scott, whose Anglican Cathedral in Liverpool was slowly and impressively rising right through the period – showed how the Gothic Revival precedents could be simplified and adapted for the many new churches needed in new suburbs. Not that Gothic had a monopoly in ecclesiastical

Above Granada Cinema, Tooting, (1931) by Cecil Masey, with interior by Theodore Komisarjevsky.

architecture, for many were in a simplified round-arched Romanesque or Byzantine style, usually in brick, which derived from the success of Westminster Cathedral. Nor were modern Gothic buildings always churches. Gothic was given a Deco flavour in Catford Town Hall, and it flourished unexpectedly inside the Granada cinema at Tooting, but above all there was George Oatley's Wills Tower for Bristol University which rose like a great cathedral in the early 1920s.

However, the most popular style in England (not Scotland) between the wars was undoubtedly Tudor. The Age of Shakespeare and Elizabeth had long had a grip on the English imagination, now further encouraged by the Korda film of *The Private Life of Henry VIII*, the first British film to achieve success across the Atlantic. Half-timbered neo-tudor houses abounded, both large and small. A diluted version of the neo-vernacular architecture of Norman Shaw and Voysey was the basis of the millions of new houses, both semi- and detached, built by house builders in the new suburbs – an important aspect of British architecture too often ignored by historians.

Sometimes, in the hands of Ernest Trobridge or Blunden Shadbolt, the half-timbering and thatch could be quite wild. The style was also used for many pubs and roadhouses. It was significant, and typical, that while the front of Liberty's store in the rebuilt Regent Street was classical, as the Crown Commissioners demanded, the building behind in Great Marlborough Street is Tudor, constructed of timbers from broken-up old ships. That it faces the Art Deco Ideal House by the American architect Raymond Hood only adds to the delightful stylistic plurality.

What is very loosely categorised as 'Art Deco' is the style now most strongly associated with the architecture and design of the inter-war decades. The name derives from the *Exposition Internationale des Arts Décoratifs* held in Paris in 1925, but the stronger influence on it came from North America. Like the Art Nouveau which preceded it, Art Deco was a style which resulted from a desire to break away from historical precedents. It was characterised by streamlining, by rounded corners, by the extravagant use of new materials and new technologies, but

Above A half-timbered pair of neo-tudor semis in Surbiton.

combined with decorative qualities and colour.
Variously described at the time as 'moderne',
'modernistic' or 'jazz modern', it was the last distinct
decorative style to evolve in Western architecture
and was much used both within and without the
new building type most characteristic of the period:
the cinema. Another, conspicuous, example was
Battersea Power Station, the work, externally, of
Giles Scott who attempted through fine brickwork to
humanise a vast industrial structure.

Art Deco buildings expressed a desire to come
to terms with the new inventions and technologies
of the new century – the motor car, aeroplanes and
an obsession with speed; transatlantic liners, radio,
the gramophone, electric power – while maintaining
traditional architectural forms and values. Such
buildings, so often commercial in function, were
despised by the advocates of a different modernity.
The austere New Architecture coming from the
Continent, defiantly flat-roofed and ostensibly
constructed of steel and concrete, was derived from
the Bauhaus and Le Corbusier and was claimed
to be truly functional. Proclaiming an extreme

Above 'By-Pass Variagted' From Osbert Lancaster's *Pillar to Post*.

Above Peter Jones Department Store by William Crabtree (1939).

headquarters of London Transport above St James's Park Station: stripped American classicism in stone over a steel frame by Charles Holden. Second came Battersea Power Station. But top came a Modern Movement building: the Peter Jones department store in Sloane Square with its curtain wall of glass wrapping around corners which was strongly influenced by the stores designed earlier in Germany by Erich Mendelsohn. But a different, and more diverse picture is presented by the book published in 1946 illustrating *Recent English Architecture 1920–1940* selected by the Architecture Club. Almost every style and building type was represented, but the image chosen for the cover was of the huge and dramatic brick ziggurat with Deco detailing at Woodside designed by Herbert Rowse to serve as a ventilating tower for the road tunnel under the River Mersey. It is as representative a building as any.

Attitudes to inter-war architecture have certainly changed since 1979; today the best examples are widely admired and it is post-war architecture that tends to be threatened. The sudden, pre-emptive demolition in 1980 of the Firestone Factory, one of several new factories in an American modernistic style, led to a reappraisal, resulting in the mass-listing of a wide variety of inter-war buildings the following year – not least Battersea Power Station (the Society's longest running case). The Society's early campaigns included one to protect Giles Gilbert Scott's clever classical red telephone boxes from extinction. Another was to prevent the gratuitous spoiling of Underground stations. The campaign whose outcome I most regret was that for Monkton, the Lutyens house in Sussex transformed into a unique Surrealist fantasy by the patron and collector Edward James, for we failed to prevent the dispersal of its contents. Had we succeeded it would surely now be treasured as a major monument, if untypical, of inter-war culture.

My own attitudes have certainly changed, as I find the Modern Movement much more interesting than I did in 1979, when it represented a blinkered hegemony which had to be challenged. But I still cannot like or admire the structure that replaced Sir Edwin Cooper's Lloyd's.

notion of progress, it arrived in England in 1924 with a house in Northampton designed by the great German architect Peter Behrens for Wenman Bassett-Lowke, who had earlier commissioned C.R. Mackintosh. A few English architects, like Maxwell Fry, followed, but the prominent Modern Movement architects were either colonials, like Connell & Ward and Coates, or from the Continent, notably Goldfinger, Lubetkin, and those refugees from Nazi Germany, Mendelsohn and Gropius. Most of their executed buildings were houses, some provoking opposition, but Mendelsohn, with the English-educated Chermayeff, was responsible for one larger masterpiece, of European importance, which was the De La Warr Pavilion at Bexhill on Sea. But it can be argued that the comparatively few Modern Movement buildings of the 1930s in Britain, glamorous as they may initially have seemed, have been greatly exaggerated in importance owing to the coverage they received in various influential architectural journals.

How, then, to make sense of the architectural confusion and variety of the period 1914–39? In the latter year, the *Architects' Journal* conducted a survey called 'Scoreboard' by asking writers, artists and celebrities to vote for what they thought were the best modern buildings. Third came 55 Broadway, the

78 Derngate

Architect: Charles Rennie Mackintosh (remodelled)
Location: 78 Derngate, Northampton
Type: Housing
Listed Grade II*

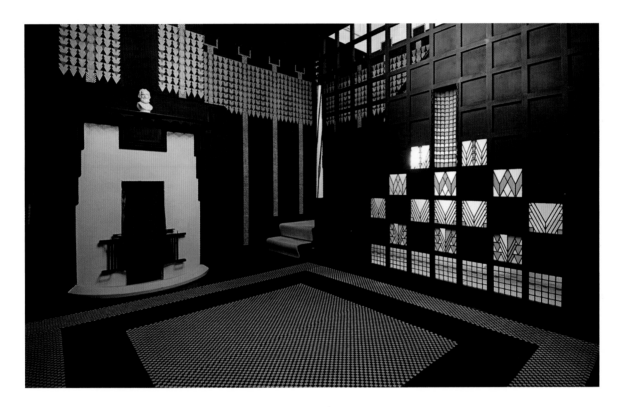

78 Derngate, a terraced house in Northampton, was dramatically remodelled into a building of international importance by the Glasgow architect, Charles Rennie Mackintosh. Commissioned by the thoroughly modern businessman W. J. Bassett-Lowke, 78 Derngate was the only English house Mackintosh designed which came to fruition.

Mackintosh's alterations begin with an impressive front door leading directly into the hall/lounge. This is an entrance designed to impress. The overall scheme is black and yellow with the walls decorated in a striking stencil of stylised trees complemented by a stair screen containing panels of decorative leaded glass.

The guest bedroom is the second dazzling showpiece of the house. Black and white stripes bordered with blue run up the walls and across the ceiling. The furniture is edged in a black band stencilled with small blue squares.

The extension to the back of this extraordinary house has been seen as a precursor to the Modern Movement.

Trustees of 78 Derngate

(1920) # Cenotaph

Architect: Sir Edwin Lutyens
Location: Whitehall, London
Type: Monument
Listed Grade II*

The Cenotaph is arguably the most important work of architecture erected in Britain in our period as it is a national shrine, the memorial to the dead of two world wars. It is also the work that brought England's greatest 20th-century architect, Sir Edwin Lutyens, to wide public recognition. The history of its genesis is curious as, despite all the grand schemes for national memorials proposed during and after the Great War of 1914–18, this modest memorial began as a temporary structure of wood and plaster erected for the Peace Day celebrations of July 1919. Lutyens had been asked rapidly to design a 'catafalque', but he proposed instead a 'cenotaph', a memorial to someone buried elsewhere, and designed a sarcophagus supported by a tall pylon, subtly modelled with his characteristic alternate setbacks. This seemingly simple, elegant structure unexpectedly became the focus of grief for a nation in mourning for its war dead, so the demand arose that it be re-erected in stone, and the permanent Cenotaph was unveiled on Armistice Day 1920. And so well did it fulfil its melancholy function that all that was required after the Second World War was to add two more dates.

Gavin Stamp

(1921)

Durlocks housing

Architect: Culpin and Bowers
Location: Folkestone, Kent
Type: Housing

Built for Sir Philip Sassoon, MP, as low cost housing for rent, the 'Durlocks' was planned on garden city principles. The 33 houses had to contend with a steeply sloping site and Sir Philip's desire that they should complement his recently completed country house at Port Lympne (now the safari park) by Herbert Baker, newly returned from South Africa – hence the slightly 'Cape Dutch' feel to the gables. Culpin and Bowers were well known through the 1920s for their public housing projects. Ewart G. Culpin, the senior partner, was both a successful journalist and an active member of the Labour Party; he was later an MP and chair of the London County Council. As secretary of the Garden City Association from 1906, he revolutionised the Garden City movement (founding the International Garden Cities and Town Planning Association) and extended its influence into all aspects of contemporary town planning, particularly the housing estates built in the years after the First World War in response to Lloyd George's 'Homes for Heroes' programme.

Ian McInnes

152 Slough Lane

Architect: Ernest George Trobridge
Location: Kingsbury, Brent, Greater London
Type: Housing/offices
Listed Grade II

Of the 4 million houses built in the inter-war years, 2.9 million were constructed by private builders, including 400,000 erected with state subsidies, 2.5 million were semis. How many were in the mock-Tudor style remains unknown.

Curiously indefinable is the work of Belfast-born Trobridge (1884–1942), the son of a painter and a disciple of Emanuel Swedenborg, who inspired his sense of proportion and the balance between architecture and nature. He chose green elm for building quickly and cheaply; a model house was the surprise of the 1920 Ideal Home exhibition. He bought a site at Kingsbury, but prices collapsed and he built only ten houses. In 1922 he moved into Hayland, to which he added Midcot in 1928, with lead lights and thatched roofs, and an inglenook. Nos. 142 and 148 Slough Lane of 1921–2 contribute to a quirky group and remind us that Middlesex was then still heavily wooded.

Elain Harwood

1923 House in the Clouds

Architect: Frederick Forbes
Location: Thorpeness, Suffolk
Type: Housing
Listed Grade II

Thorpeness was developed as a private fantasy holiday village in the 1920s by a Scottish barrister, Glencairn Stuart Ogilvie. The most outlandish building, the Gazebo or 'House in the Clouds', was built as a water tank. Water was pumped by a neighbouring windmill rescued from nearby Aldringham, and the tower beneath the fake 'house' contained a dwelling with unrivalled views. Structural support comes from steel joists and concrete made from Thorpeness sand, but the weatherboarding and pantile roof connect it to the Suffolk landscape.

When it was dubbed a 'monstrous pigeoncote' by the *Sunday Referee*, Ogilvie replied it was 'more practical and more picturesque than those usually erected by our municipal authorities [and] might be copied in all modern town planning'. Symbol of the whimsical vision for Thorpeness and one of the strangest houses in England, the House in the Clouds continues to enchant and can be rented for a unique holiday.

Charlotte de Mille

1924　Taunton School Science Building

Architect: E Vincent Harris
Location: Staplegrove Road, Taunton, Somerset
Type: Education
Listed Grade II

Harris completed this late English Renaissance block, which included a Memorial Hall, in 1924. It was encased in Bath stone with mullioned and transomed windows all round. The memorial function was announced by a small central entrance block with Gothic door and oriel window above, contrasting with the learning blocks arranged either side. The war memorial is a large open space in the centre of the internal rear wall. Corridors lead to the classrooms off to left and right. The ground and first floor are linked by a double staircase, work rooms on both floors being a mixture of laboratories, lecture rooms, library, staff rooms and stores. John Brown (c.1928) said 'the memorial aspect of the structure [is] wonderfully observed and maintained by the architect.'

Nicholas Holmes

1925

Wills Memorial Building

Architect: Sir George Oatley
Location: Queen's Road, Bristol
Type: Education
Listed Grade II*

The Wills Memorial Building is the last great Gothic secular building to be built in this country. It was designed by Bristol's most important architect of the twentieth century, Sir George Herbert Oatley, in 1912. But because of the outbreak of the First World War it was not completed until 1925. It was paid for by George and Henry Wills of tobacco company fame (or infamy), in memory of their father Henry Overton Wills III. He had enabled the foundation of Bristol University in 1909 with a gift of £100,000.

The Wills brothers wanted to create 'an architectural elevation at once worthy of the University and an ornament to our native city'. Oatley continued and developed the Gothic tradition and combined it with practical planning and modern construction methods (it is of reinforced concrete faced with Bath stone) to produce a building perfectly suited to its purpose. The monumental 215-feet-high perpendicular Gothic tower is now as much a symbol of Bristol as Brunel's Clifton Suspension Bridge, and Bristolians cannot imagine Park Street without it at the top.

Sarah Whittingham

1926 Shredded Wheat Factory

Architect: Louis de Soissons
Location: Welwyn Garden City, Hertfordshire
Type: Industrial
Listed Grade II

My choice is Louis de Soissons's 1926 complex for Nabisco, the Shredded Wheat factory. The ranked silos and spreading sheds alongside the railway track in Welwyn Garden City have always fascinated me, glimpsed almost kinetically from the train windows. American companies, drawn by innovation, were quicker off the mark to move into Ebenezer Howard's radical 'cities' (another example being Spirella at Letchworth, built 1912–20). Here, long before I'd learned that Le Corbusier had published the grain stores of the American Midwest prairies as the epitome of modern form following function, was an anglicised version, a cathedral in a leafy Beaux-Arts planned town.

What I did not know when I proposed it is that the sheds have now been razed, leaving the Grade II listed elements (notably the silos) standing beached on a vast apron of vacant land. In January 2012, Welwyn Hatfield Council refused Tesco's application for redevelopment. There was no appeal and since then the remaining buildings have fallen increasingly derelict.

Gillian Darley

1927

Scottish National War Memorial

Architect: Sir Robert Lorimer
Location: Edinburgh Castle, Edinburgh
Type: Monument
Listed Grade A

The Scottish National War Memorial is one of the outstanding pieces of public art of its time. A shrine to the nation's collective loss, it commemorates all the individual men and women of Scotland who fell in the Great War and is the masterpiece of its architect, Sir Robert Lorimer. Leading a team of 200 artists and craftsmen, Lorimer designed the building in a style inspired by the architecture of Renaissance Scotland to include monuments to all the Services, regiments and corps that served in the war, but also to the many non-combatants and uniquely to all Scottish women. The outstanding stained glass by Douglas Strachan and the bronze frieze by Alice and Morris Meredith Williams, together with the numerous other sculptures do more than gather diverse monuments in one place, however. They also present the wider message of hope that the terrible sacrifice of the Great War should not have been in vain: that it would secure peace and should prove truly to have been 'the war to end war.'

Duncan Macmillan

1928

Firestone Factory

Architect: Wallis, Gilbert and Partners
Location: Great West Road, Brentford, London
Type: Commercial/offices
Demolished

Every conservation society needs a martyr – a demolition so outrageous and shocking that the press and public realise the need for the society. With the Georgian Group, it was the Adelphi; with the Victorian Society, the Euston Arch. For the Twentieth Century Society (then the Thirties Society) the Firestone Factory became its martyr in 1980.

Wallis, Gilbert and Partners designed it, and the Hoover Factory (1932), in the style now known as Art Deco but then called jazz modern or moderne. At the time, the influential *Architectural Review* championed the Modern Movement and the moderne style was anathema. By 1979, when Marcus Binney and Simon Jenkins asked me to join them in founding the society, this view was in retreat. Ornament had begun to seem a tempting alternative to barebones functionalism and the New Brutalism.

The Firestone Building was a distinguished example of Art Deco, built for the American tyre manufacturers, the Firestone Tire and Rubber Company of Akron, Ohio; and the design of the whole building, not just the façade, was based on that of an Egyptian temple.

When they decided to cease production in Brentford, they sold the land for development. A call from the Department of the Environment to the developers (but not to us) alerted them that the minister, Michael Heseltine, was going to list the building on Tuesday; on Sunday bulldozers were sent in to demolish the façade. It was a calculated act of philistinism. Simon Jenkins wrote in the first Thirties Society Journal: 'I can recall few buildings […] whose destruction has produced more spontaneous outrage from laymen.'

Just afterwards, senior civil servant Brian Anthony 'serendipitously knocked on Heseltine's door and came up with a plan to prevent the Firestone debacle from happening again' (*The Times*); one of his triumphs was to save the Hoover Factory. That would probably not have happened but for the martyrdom of the Firestone.

Bevis Hillier

(1929) William Booth Memorial College

Architect: Sir Giles Gilbert Scott, acting as associate architect with Gordon and Viner
Location: Denmark Hill, London
Type: Education

Scott's college soars above Denmark Hill station and the Georgian and Victorian terraces of Camberwell where I live. Camberwell has been called the original garden city, in the sense that it was a city built in people's gardens. When the great Regency villas that dotted the area were demolished in the last century institutions wanting to expand moved south of the river. The college was one, conceived as a practical monument to the Salvation Army's founder William Booth.

It has a family resemblance to Scott's more famous works: the dominant central tower with the low ranges to either side echo Cambridge University Library and, to a lesser extent, Bankside Power Station. But unlike its eminent siblings it has a certain modesty. The plain brick with its little froth of Gothic detail, like braid on a Salvationist's uniform, makes it a building of which, despite its massiveness, its neighbours have grown fond.

Rosemary Hill

Odeon Cinema

Architect: William Illingworth
Location: Godwin Street, Bradford
Type: Entertainment

Bradford was a hair's breadth away from losing its 84-year-old Odeon building. Even though it now stands as an empty and increasingly scruffy bookend to the popular City Park, Bradfordians have always had a soft spot for the twin-domed, red brick former cinema and ballroom.

The city centre landmark was earmarked for demolition only a few years ago to make way for a largely unwanted office scheme. Fortunately, as the downturn bit, its unwelcome replacement became financially unviable and was eventually scrapped in late 2012. The ex-cinema eventually transferred to the council for just £1 and bidders are now vying to bring it back to life. Designed by William Illingworth, the chunky Italian Renaissance-style building was the first cinema in Britain to be purpose-built for 'talkies' and, although it was bashed about internally before closing in 2000, it has proved remarkably resilient. Urban explorers have discovered that some of its original Art Deco features and ceilings remain intact – albeit hidden. Bradford is a city of domes and the Odeon's copper-topped cupolas are still among its most loved.

Richard Waite

1931

India Buildings, Liverpool

Architect: Herbert Rowse with Briggs and Thornely
Location: India Buildings, Water Street, Liverpool
Type: Commercial/offices
Listed Grade II*

·WATER·STREET·ELEVATION·
Scale ⅛ inch equals 1 foot

A confident nine-storey, neo-classical, Portland stone clad competition winner, designed with Rowse's typically stylish flair, India Buildings were built for the Alfred Holt shipping line. Liverpool then was a thriving world port, looking New York in the eye. Charles Reilly wrote: 'the building would not disgrace Fifth Avenue'. Its best feature is the glossy arcade of finely detailed shops which pierces the building. Each detail (Bromsgrove Guild lamps, bronze post box, plaques) is Rowseingly perfect. Rowse proudly asserted, 'Never present an alternative; it shows you have not solved your problem.' When the Passport Office moved out, the Buildings declined under new owners but recent upgrading to II*, promoted by C20 Society, might stimulate sympathetic regeneration; Rowse's genius deserves no less.

Aidan Turner-Bishop

Boots D10 (Wets) Building

Architect: Owen Williams
Location: off Humber Road South, Beeston, Nottinghamshire
Type: Commercial/offices
Listed Grade 1

The factory is also known as Boots Packed Wet Goods Factory. Built in 1930–32 for the Boots Company it is one of several fine buildings on this large site, and as such has achieved international recognition, and was listed in 1971. Engineer Sir Owen Williams, the designer, is also known for the *Daily Express* building in Manchester, 1936–9 (listed Grade II* in 1974) considered to be his finest work.

The D10 building was notable for its innovative use and development of structural concrete. It used reinforced concrete, the structural frame, as an external material, allowing the design to incorporate unusually large areas of glass. It is the earliest use of such a structural system in a large-scale industrial building in England. The building is huge – 580 feet long and over 70 feet in height. A railway ran through the centre of the factory, enabling raw materials to be delivered and finished products taken away.

David Rock

Battersea Power Station

Architect: Sir Giles Gilbert Scott
Location: 188 Kirtling Street, London
Type: Industrial
Listed Grade II*

Thanks to the involvement of a distinguished architect, Battersea Power Station became the first electricity generating station to receive public acclaim. The original proposal for a large coal-burning facility on the south bank of the Thames, designed by the engineer Leonard Pearce and the Manchester architects Halliday and Agate, aroused strong opposition from residents in Chelsea and Westminster. So a knighted architect was wheeled in to allay fears in the shape of Giles Gilbert Scott, admired as the architect of Liverpool Cathedral. Scott carefully modelled the bases of the four column-like chimneys and detailed the superb brickwork of the vast walls in a non-historicist 'jazz modern' manner. The result was that when Battersea 'A' with its two chimneys was completed in 1933, it was praised as a dramatic, modern 'cathedral of power'. Battersea 'B' followed later, and for a while the station was a 'three-pin plug' until the fourth chimney went up in 1955. Finally made redundant in 1983, Battersea Power Station has been the Society's longest-running case, and it is deplorable that the dramatic view of the building from the adjacent railway viaduct will be lost under the current development proposals for the wider site.

Gavin Stamp

Above Aerial photo of the station taken
in 1950 showing the construction of the
final chimney that formed part of the later
Battersea B Power Station and give the well-
recogniseed four-chimney layout of today.

Right The surviving interior of control room
A at the power station.

Opposite Battersea Power Station
chimneystack operating in the 1930s.

(1934) Lawn Road Flats

Architect: Wells Wintemute Coates for Rosemary and Jack Pritchard
Location: Lawn Road, Belsize Park, London
Type: Housing
Listed Grade I

There it presides in Lawn Road. A pinky-cream painted block of flats with extravagantly cantilevered balconies, it stands as a built reproach to the older forms of domestic architecture it overlooks.

Completed in 1934, this was a determined attempt to re-cast architecture in the light of the new realities of domestic life and urban living that had emerged since the First World War, but which had hitherto not been given satisfying form. Together clients and architect created a rigorously planned and intricately serviced environment in which those who had previously been unable to feel 'at home' now could; an experience which the block's recent renovation now brings to a new generation of residents. But it is much more than a feat of problem-solving. Coates's utmost mastery of materials, space and form (and this his first complete building) and their synthesis into a distinctive language of architecture make this a real turning point in the development of English modernism.

Elizabeth Darling

De La Warr Pavilion

Architect: Erich Mendelsohn and Serge Chermayeff
Location: Bexhill-on-Sea, East Sussex
Type: Entertainment
Listed Grade I

It is one of history's fabulous freaks that a major example of modern architecture queens it over a minor south coast resort. Germany's loss was England's gain when Mendelsohn escaped to London, and Thomas Tait's bold competition choice led to the first public building this side of the Channel to demonstrate the new architecture with life-enhancing verve. Chermayeff's interiors, within a welded steel frame by Felix Samuely, gave substance to the vision.

It is luckier still that when the Pavilion had metaphorically got stuck in bedroom slippers and curlers in the 1990s, a local enthusiast, Jill Theis, became a local councillor with a mission to recover its youth, leading to John McAslan's refurbishment in 2004–5, and its new direction as an arts venue combined with a community facility. There is nothing more uplifting than to spend a day there watching the rain or the sun as it arcs round from Hastings to Beachy Head.

Alan Powers

1936 Simpson's Piccadilly

Architect: Joseph Emberton
Location: 203–206 Piccadilly, London
Type: Commercial/offices
Listed Grade II*

Simpson's was an ongoing case for the C20 Society when I first joined the Society and the fact that it is now Waterstones' flagship store demonstrates the success and longevity of Emberton's 1930s design. Primarily a men's outfitters, Simpson's pioneered 'the smart ready-made two piece suit and Daks self-supporting trousers', but by the 1970s the shop was old fashioned, and is said to have inspired the TV comedy 'Are You Being Served?'

John McAslan's refurbishment demonstrates that Emberton's building could be put to 21st-century use with little modification. This is partially due to Felix Samuely's innovative, electrically welded steel structural frame, which allows an open floor plan.

The C20 Society was concerned that Ashley Havinden's signage should not be lost, and when Waterstones first took over the store the lettering was in the original Havinden style. This can still be seen on the Jermyn Street entrance. Unfortunately the main signage has now been replaced by the Waterstones corporate style.

Cela Selley

Greenside

Architect: Connell, Ward and Lucas
Location: Chestnut Avenue, Virginia Water, Surrey
Type: Housing
Demolished

Greenside was a fine example of an early flat-roofed Modern Movement house, by one of the most innovative firms of the decade. A Grade II listed building, it was demolished without consent in 2003 by its owner, who argued that the Human Rights Act justified his action. The C20 Society had argued that the building could be restored, fought the owner at a public inquiry, and successfully called for his criminal prosecution. The Inspector upheld our case and the owner was convicted of a criminal offence. Although the fines levied against him were small in comparison to the potential value of a cleared site in such a prestigious location (immediately adjacent to the 17th green of the Wentworth Golf Course), the sentence was an important deterrent. Critically, the Inspector recognised that listed buildings controls are not a disproportionate burden on building owners, and so dismissed the Human Rights Act defence, which would have undermined conservation.

We have subsequently campaigned for more realistic fines in such cases, and support and publicise the growing number of examples of buildings where creature comforts and environmental performance have been upgraded effectively and sympathetically.

Catherine Croft

Above left The north front of Greenside
in Surrey, originally called Bracken, showing
entrance and staircase tower.

Above The first floor living room on the
south front.

1938 Finsbury Health Centre

Architect: Berthold Lubetkin and Tecton
Location: Pine Street, London
Type: Healthcare
Listed Grade I

Finsbury Health Centre was arguably modern architecture's most important single achievement in England in the first half of the 20th century. This realisation of a radical humanitarian brief for a deprived community in a new building-type encapsulated all modernism's progressive ideals – social, technical, aesthetic – with a political and architectural conviction unequalled by any other work of its era, anticipating the foundation of the National Health Service by a clear decade. Of particular concern to architect and client alike was to create a welcoming ambiance that would overcome the apprehension and intimidation typically associated with traditional hospital environments. As Lubetkin once told me, 'the curving façade and outstretched arms were intended to introduce a smile into what in fact is a machine.' The smile has been reciprocated. The Centre is deeply loved by its staff and patients despite years of inadequate maintenance and it remains an indispensable healthcare facility for its local community. The Finsbury Health Centre Preservation Trust has recently been formed to work for its full restoration.

John Allan

1939

Impington Village College

Architect: Walter Gropius
Location: New Road, Impington, Cambridgeshire
Type: Education
Listed Grade I

The remarkable Grade I listed building of Impington Village College was born from the meeting of two visionary thinkers. Founder of the Bauhaus at Dessau, Walter Gropius fled Nazi Germany in 1934 when he came to London to join an architectural partnership with Maxwell Fry. At the same time the innovative educationalist Henry Morris was negotiating investment and land to build three new Village Colleges in Cambridgeshire.

Morris believed that the village college building should act as 'the silent teacher', offering a welcoming and inspiring space for local communities to learn and socialise. When he met Gropius in 1934 there was no doubt in his mind as to who should design the buildings at Impington. Gropius' radical plan brought new consideration for the social impact of the built environment, and laid out a model for school and community buildings that has since been replicated around the world. The British history of architecture professor Sir Nikolaus Pevsner describes Impington Village College as 'one of the best buildings of its date in England, if not the best'. Today as I sit in this stunning building, I am inspired by the vision of these great men whose ideologies are as relevant now as they were 75 years ago.

Amy Wormald

1940

No. 4 Boathouse

Architect: E A Scott
Location: Portsmouth Historic Dockyard, Portsmouth
Type: Industrial

No. 4 Boathouse is a product of the rapid rearmament in the late 1930s, and a rare example of an inter-war heavy engineering shop, the latest in a continuous chain of dockyard structures surviving in Portsmouth from the 17th to the 20th centuries. It was designed for the maintenance and fitting out of small boats up to 40 tons, and constructed of reinforced concrete with a riveted steel frame, a saw tooth roof profile and facades designed with reference to contemporary American factories.

The Boathouse's finest hour was as one of only two locations where assault landing craft were manufactured for the D-Day landings, and the site for the modification and testing of experimental landing craft design.

This magnificent building, which I have described as 'functionalism on a heroic scale', was saved from demolition after a campaign by SAVE Britain's Heritage. SAVE secured a reprieve from an application for demolition, and working with architect Huw Thomas, drew up proposals for its reuse as a centre for displaying small boats of the fleet.

Marcus Binney

1941 St Peter's Church

Architect: Cyril Farey
Location: Vera Avenue, Grange Park, London
Type: Place of worship

I've known this church and its wooden church hall – the original temporary church, now demolished – for the past 25 years. Built during the Second World War, Farey's church caused controversy in the local press at the time, but it's a great example of architectural salvage. It's said that no new timber was used in the construction, all of it coming from London churches destroyed during the Blitz. Pews, font and choir stalls were also rescued and the church bell, dated 1785, came from St John's, Drury Lane.

Architect Cyril Farey is better known for his perspectivist architectural drawings. In the 1920s he worked with Edwin Lutyens and at one time the architectural room at the Royal Academy was so full of Farey perspectives that Lutyens called it 'the Farey Glen'.

St Peter's brick-built exterior, with rectangular windows, parapets and pantiles looks Scandinavian-classical, whilst the white-plastered interior has Romanesque influence. This church demonstrates that Farey could build as well as draw.

Cela Selley

1942

Wythenshawe Bus Garage

Architect: G. Noel Hill, Manchester City Architect's Department
Location: Harling Road, Northenden, Manchester
Type: Transport
Listed Grade II*

Wythenshawe is Manchester's garden suburb, created in the 1920s but never connected to the city's tram network. Instead it was served by a ragtag of public and private bus services. A new garage was eventually built, but it was immediately commandeered by the Ministry of Aircraft Production for building Lancaster bombers and was released only in 1946. Resembling a grey whale beached in an industrial estate, the drama of the interior is wholly unexpected.

Wythenshawe's concrete arches have a span of 165 feet and are 42 feet high. The innovation is that the concrete shell roof between them is just 2¾ inches thick, a technique brought from Germany in the 1930s. More examples followed in the 1950s for schools, factories, and especially for bus garages as trams were replaced everywhere. Here aeroplanes have had the last laugh; the building now garages the cars of holidaymakers using nearby Ringway Airport.

Elain Harwood

1943

D Block, Bletchley Park

Architect: Ministry of Works and Buildings
Location: Bletchley Park, Buckinghamshire
Type: Military
Listed Grade II

Heroic things sometimes happen in the most banal settings. D Block, its bungalow wings laid out off one long corridor in a 'spider' plan, is more substantial than Bletchley Park's earlier wooden huts. It has steel reinforcement and a concrete roof, so might have survived a near miss. Happily for the struggle to rid Europe of fascism – which at times appeared nearly lost – Bletchley Park was never bombed. D Block was the setting of the industrial-scale interception and decrypting of war-time messages. In 2014 the wooden huts are undergoing restoration and D Block is next in line. Three shifts of staff each of up to 700 people worked 24 hours a day in D Block alone, bussed in from their small-town billets across Buckinghamshire. Nearly all women, hardly any D Block staff knew what the millions of messages and decrypts they were handling meant, or why they were important. Most were banal, serving merely to indicate the enemy's usual patterns of operation from which strategic changes might be deduced. The brilliance of the Bletchley mathematicians, their cracking of Enigma, the creation of the world's first electronic programmable computer on the site – all have captured the world's imagination. But for me, D Block and its routine and dutiful drudgery is as worthy of remembering.

Roland Jeffery

Italian Chapel, Lamb Holm

Architect: Italian Prisoners of War
Location: Lamb Holm, Orkney
Type: Place of worship
Listed Grade A

On October 14, 1939, HMS *Royal Oak* was sunk by a German submarine in Scapa Flow and 834 men died. Churchill ordered the construction of protective barriers. Italian Prisoners of War, based in Camp 60, worked constructing the Barriers. Led by Domenico Chiocchetti, and encouraged by their padre and the British commander, the Italians improved their drab camp. They constructed an elaborately decorated chapel, using two Nissen huts, with scrap materials transformed by skilled artists, electricians and metal workers. Statues, trompe l'oeil paintings, coloured glass windows and a decorated façade were created. Work was completed by 1944.

After the war the camp closed and the chapel declined. It was restored, by Chiocchetti and the islanders, in 1961 and listed Grade A in 1987. It's now a popular tourist site: testament to the prisoners' skills and our common human need to embellish and worship.

Aidan Turner-Bishop

Waterloo Bridge

Architect: Sir Giles Gilbert Scott
Location: London SE1
Type: Transport
Listed Grade II*

The views from Waterloo Bridge have to be the best in London – a great sweeping arc from the South Bank, the London Eye, the Houses of Parliament and the Victoria Embankment to Somerset House, St Paul's Cathedral and the National Theatre. The bridge has an elegant simplicity – a suave mid-20th century modern creation by the great Sir Giles Gilbert Scott working with engineers Rendel, Palmer and Tritton. The five arches of the 80-feet-wide bridge are constructed of reinforced concrete and faced with Portland stone resting on boat-shaped cutwaters of granite. It was commissioned by the London County Council to replace its much-loved but structurally unsound and far too narrow Georgian predecessor, by Sir John Rennie, of 1817. The present-day Waterloo Bridge was opened in December 1945 by the then Deputy Prime Minister Herbert Morrison who, as Leader of the London County Council in 1934, had approved its construction. During the Second World War much of the building work was carried out by women, earning it the nickname 'The Ladies Bridge'.

Edmund Bird

1946 Excalibur Estate

Architect: Uni-Seco
Location: 17 Meliot Road, London
Type: Housing

17 Meliot Road is a 'Uni-Seco' prefab on the Excalibur Estate, one of 185 on the UK's largest post-war prefab estate. Thousands of prefabs were built across bombed-out London (of 156,623 over the country) after the Second World War to alleviate the housing shortage for returning servicemen and their families. Since then, most have been knocked down, and the Excalibur Estate is set to be bulldozed and replaced by modern housing within the next few years.

The estate was built in 1946 by German and Italian Prisoners of War. It was supposed to last ten years, but almost 70 years later, it's still standing and this house was lived in and cherished until last autumn. The two-bed council houses had immersion heaters, built-in cupboards, indoor bathroom, constant hot water, separate indoor toilets, and a spacious garden, offering unheard-of luxury and comfort. 'To find a bathroom inside was magic', recalls Mr O'Mahony, who has lived on the Estate since the end of the war, 'and a refrigerator! Ordinary people didn't have them.'

Temporarily a Prefab Museum, 17 Meliot Road is welcoming the public in 2014 to discover this amazing bungalow and slice of 20th-century social history that will soon disappear for good.

Elisabeth Blanchet

1947 — Somerford Grove Estate

Architect: Frederick Gibberd (with Borough Engineer G L Downing)
Location: Hackney, London
Type: Housing

The Somerford Grove Estate occupies 9 acres of land cleared for development following the war. Built in the Metropolitan Borough of Hackney between 1947 and 1949, the post-war estate breaks from the existing pattern of long straight streets lined with two- and three-storey terraced houses. Instead, Frederick Gibberd grouped the new buildings to form a series of closes and courtyards, each with their own character; axial views across the site are contrasted with these more intimate enclosed spaces. The landscape and floorscape are designed to create visual interest – the latter designed to correspond with the facades of the buildings. The scheme is certainly a pioneering example of post-war 'visual planning'.

Comprising a mixture of three- and four-storey modern flats, terraced houses and bungalows with gardens and pitched roofs, the scheme can be seen as an exemplar of 'mixed development', as well as an important contribution to English post-war modernism.

Christine Hui Lan Manley

St Teresa's Bakery and Store, Dingle's Department Store

Architect: Gordon Tait of Sir John Burnet, Tait and Lorne
Location: Beaumont Road, Plymouth
Type: Retail

The first new building to be completed in Plymouth after the war, this was designed by Gordon Tait, who was demobbed early from the RAF to assist his father, Thomas S. Tait in the revived London office. The four-storey building was steel-framed and clad in precast concrete planks of Portland stone aggregate as suggested in Patrick Abercrombie's 1943 *A Plan for Plymouth*. In its details – the stair tower of 2-inch Dutch brick, the porthole and horizontal metal windows – it refers back to many of the firm's buildings of the 1930s, but in its unashamedly horizontal composition, the projecting eaves and the pioneering cladding it looks forward to the 'lighter' compositions of the 1950s. The bright future is symbolised by the cornucopia cast into the concrete panels.

The Bakery became disused in the 1970s and shops were inserted but by the 1990s the whole building was derelict. In the early 2000s it was converted into student flats. Following refusal of an application for listing, the single-storey bakery was demolished and a floor added to the four-storey block. The original building is now unrecognisable.

Jeremy Gould

Windmill Green

Architect: Tayler and Green,
Location: Ditchingam, Norfolk
Type: Housing
Listed Grade II

'An attempt to entrap the whole of East Anglian space in one great gesture. It is a kind of oath of allegiance to the landscape...' wrote Ian Nairn about this early scheme by the masters of the rural council house, Tayler and Green, a partnership based in Lowestoft. Tayler hated the effect of standard semi-detached pairs of houses like 'a row of pointed teeth with alternate teeth extracted.'

Three ranges are set at an open angle around a large green, with clear views to the country on the western side, until insensitively infilled. Nowhere else did Tayler and Green build such long terraces, in homage to Ernst May's Frankfurt Siedlungen. The problem of access to back gardens was solved with their invention of covered passageways for each house; different coloured fronts relieved monotony, while front gardens and wicket gates encouraged personal display.

Alan Powers

1950 Templewood Primary School

Architect: Hertfordshire County Council
Location: Welwyn Garden City, Hertfordshire
Type: Education
Listed Grade II*

Templewood belongs to the little crop of Hertfordshire's post-war primary schools built at the precious moment when the experiment of prefabrication buildings in series was still fresh but had gone far enough to produce architecture of real cleverness, sensitivity and flexibility. Far from the ponderous rigidity of later prefabrication, Templewood represents an instrument for child-centred education which is delicate and miraculously timeless. Low yet light and serene shared spaces, standard square classrooms planned in staggered order so as to give them light from two sides, and charming works of art – all part of the humane Hertfordshire package – combine with a bosky garden-city site to make this the best of these schools today.

The job-architect for Templewood was Cleeve Barr, who had given up banking and become a communist and architect because he wanted to do something useful. He had flown Caravelles to Russia during the war, and it is not by chance that Russian fairy tales are the topic of the murals by Pat Tew, recently and admirably restored. Architect and painter would have regarded Templewood as socialism in action. As for Le Corbusier, when he visited the school he aptly remarked 'C'est jolie'.

Andrew Saint

Royal Festival Hall

Architect: Robert Matthew and J L Martin with Peter Moro and the London County Council
Location: Belvedere Road, London
Type: Entertainment
Listed Grade I

It is hard now to believe how disdainful many architects once were about the design style of the Festival Hall. The Thirties Society first lobbied for listing it in 1983, and once it was included in the first batch of post-war listings in 1988, its stock with the wider public began to rise. The decorative Festival style acted as a soft way in for non-architects to understand and appreciate other kinds of modernism, a trend that helped the C20 Society mature and reach a wider public. One of the best things about the Festival Hall is its function as a people's palace, or free clubhouse for anyone and everyone.

During the 1990s, however, the foyer spaces became increasingly cluttered with retail and cafés. The best part of Allies and Morrison's refurbishment of 2004–7 was to return some clarity, but the concert hall interior lost some of its authenticity in the search for better acoustics.

Alan Powers

Post-war Architecture
Elain Harwood

The Thirties Society changed its name to the Twentieth Century Society (C20 Society) in 1992 because post-war buildings were taking up an increasing part of its casework and events programme. The press officer at Peter Moro's Nottingham Playhouse of 1961–1963 was utterly bemused that the Thirties Society should want to visit, and it took ages to explain that our interest was in the whole period after 1914.

Most of the first serious post-war cases were in London: the National Union of Mineworkers' (NUM) headquarters on the Euston Road, by Moiret and Wood, whose fine artworks were taken by Arthur Scargill to Barnsley; James Gowan's Schreiber House of 1963–4 in Hampstead, its later pool house threatened by redevelopment; and Albert Richardson's Bracken House of 1955–9, up for demolition. In 1987 this became the first post-war building in England to be listed; with postmodernism at its height it was unsurprising if ironic that this honour should go to a classical building ridiculed on its completion. Already, however, Cadw had listed the thoroughly modern Brynmawr Rubber Factory of 1948–52 in Wales, though this was to be

Above Brynmawr Rubber Factory by the Architects' Co-Partnership, completed in 1952 and demolished in 2002.

a Pyrrhic victory as no economic use or restoration grants were ever forthcoming, and the building was demolished in 2002.

These cases, although thrown up randomly by circumstances, perfectly demonstrate the range of buildings found in the 1950s and early 1960s. The French commonly speak of *Les Trentes Glorieuses*, three decades of unsurpassed prosperity after the Second World War. In Britain, these years are most simply understood as having three economic stages: a period of slow and intermittent growth followed by a boom (again with interruptions) in the years 1959–66, and a steady decline thereafter upset by an artificially generated growth in 1971 and a brief economic revival in 1976–7. Architectural trends follow a broadly similar pattern.

Two hundred thousand houses in Britain were lost in the war, another 250,000 were rendered uninhabitable and 3 million needed repair. About 250,000 new houses were built during the war, equivalent to a single year's supply and totally outstripped by the demands of migration and younger marriages. With the British economy debilitated by the war, sterling placed unfavourably against the dollar thanks to the Bretton Woods agreement signed in return for American aid, and shortages of building materials and labourers, post-war building began slowly. New building was controlled by building licences for materials and concentrated on housing, schools and industrial buildings, preferences enforced by taxation on the profits of redevelopment ('betterment') from 1947 that persuaded many developers to sit tight on their landholdings until the legislation was repealed in 1953. The post-war years are dominated as no others by architecture funded by the state. If the National Health Service, created in 1948, built little of value, local authorities and the new town development corporations offered opportunities for public building as never before, and the universities, autonomous public bodies with direct access to the Treasury's purse, became the most important clients of the period.

The architecture of the 1940s and 1950s was simple, sometimes ungainly in its spindly shapes and austere materials, but it was often closer in looks

Above Liverpool Metropolitan Cathedral, Frederick Gibberd (1967).

as well as spirit to the de Stijl and constructivist movements of early modernism than had been the buildings of the 1930s with their more traditional references. Winning the war had seen problems appraised from first principles, and this approach was now put to build prefabricated houses and schools, the latter more successfully thanks to larger budgets, economies of scale and a committed group of architects who came together at Hertfordshire County Council. Steel frames and concrete cladding panels were enlivened by a consciousness of the scale of their tiny clients and a programme of bright paint colours, murals and sculptures. The amalgamation of architecture, art and engineering that dominated the Festival of Britain in 1951 continued to inspire the most impressive buildings of the next decade, including not only schools and the NUM Building but projects as diverse as *Time* and *Life*'s offices or Congress House (both in London), and Coventry Cathedral.

The post-war Labour governments of 1945–51

Opposite The Barbican, designed by Chamberlin, Powell and Bon.   Above Preston Bus Station, by Building Design Partnership.

promised much but lacked the resources to deliver, though it is now easy to overlook the investment made in the coal industry (nationalised in 1947) and electricity (1948). Many local authorities and private companies had already started to build new power stations, in which investment over the 1950s approached spending on defence. The 1950s saw a steady growth in the domestic market for consumer goods, matched by the building of factories, offices and houses for private sale, especially following the end of building licences in November 1954. Public building remained limited, however, with controls on capital expenditure and loans imposed following the Suez Crisis of late 1956. Nevertheless, in July 1957 Harold Macmillan declared in a speech to his fellow Conservatives at Bedford that 'most of the people in this country have never had it so good'.

The boom time for building saw maturity, too, in the work of architects trained in the late 1930s and

1940s and who had come to prominence after the war while still young. This change can be seen in the series of designs made by Powell and Moya for additions to Brasenose College, Oxford, beginning with proposals for a simple, flat, stone building with lines of windows in 1956, and evolving over the next two years into a rich composition of projecting and receding planes, conceived with classical proportions but with a weighty battered profile and constructivist angles, and concrete was combined with traditional stone and lead claddings as never before in Britain. Most of the Oxford and Cambridge colleges had private assets to support their building campaigns, but the universities also built ambitiously thanks to five-year programmes from the University Grants Committee that allowed them to plan ahead. They, including the 19 new universities established across the UK between 1958 and 1968, were aided in their choice of architects by a handful of experts:

Above Centre Point, 1961–5 by Ricard Seifert and Partners.

John Summerson, J.M. Richards and most notably Leslie Martin, whose position as Professor of Architecture at Cambridge University and a fellow of Jesus College made him a sympathetic figure for academics seeking advice. Martin's patronage was vital to the careers of many practices within and outside university work who defined the best of 1960s architecture, including Chamberlin, Powell and Bon; Patrick Hodgkinson; Howell, Killick, Partridge and Amis; Denys Lasdun; Richard Sheppard and Partners; Alison and Peter Smithson; James Stirling, with and without James Gowan; and Colin St John Wilson. The withdrawal of the UGC from capital spending after 1967 coincided with a downturn in building as a whole.

But if less was built in the 1970s, with building times lengthened by the 'stop-go' economy, delays in securing planning permissions and shortages of materials and labour, there remains much to be enjoyed. The Society's journal, *The Seventies*, identified a great variety of architecture produced in the years 1966-79. This coherent time period (rather longer than a decade) was marked by inflation and economic instability internationally, prompted by the Vietnam and Yom Kippur wars. This was made worse in Britain by declining industries, many of which were pushed into unwieldy, semi-nationalised mega-companies; a lack of investment in training and technology; and a loss of belief in government – of which extensive strike action was one response.

Yet creativity there was, along with new ventures into computing, investment banking and much of the business support structure we have today. The office buildings of the 1970s, whether speculative like many in the City of London, or specially designed for clients like Willis Faber in Ipswich, are far closer to those of the 2010s than the 1960s. Many large housing schemes, like the Barbican, Byker and the work of LB Camden came slowly to fruition, as did the Barbican Arts Centre and National Theatre, while public libraries and museums were built in large numbers by local authorities anxious to dispose of their capital resources ahead of government reorganisation – in 1974 for most authorities outside London. It was a decade of contradiction: on the one hand of growing vandalism and violence, not least as the Irish Troubles escalated, while on the other there was greater investment in higher education and the arts than ever before or since. The buildings reflected that variety, with modernism moving into high tech and exploring new materials and techniques at the very time that other architects were turning back to traditional materials in search of energy-saving construction or postmodernism.

The growing conservation movement, as well as references to classical traditions or Art Deco, were indicative of the growing rejection to modernism in architecture, just as the post-war welfare state could no longer support the expectations made of it. The advent of Margaret Thatcher's Conservative Government in May 1979 heralded the end of capital expenditure by public bodies, and the onset of a more commercial world where the rivalry between high tech and postmodernism became still more exaggerated. Thirty years of adverse criticism, from which *Les Trentes Glorieuses* are just emerging, have scarcely dampened the richness of the best architecture of these years and it is no surprise that it continues to dominate the Society's casework.

Opposite Lambeth Towers, by George Finch, 1971.

Stockwell Bus Garage

Architect: Adie, Button and Partners
Location: Binfield Road, London
Type: Transport
Listed Grade II*

Stockwell Bus Garage, opened on 2nd April 1952, was designed to hold up to 200 vehicles serving a variety of central and south west London routes.

Listed Grade II* in 1988, it is one of the finest examples of post war modernist architecture, and follows directly on from the Dome of Discovery at the Festival of Britain in the preceding year. London Transport, into which the Underground Group of Companies had been assumed in 1933, had a proud tradition of ensuring that form followed function in an elegant style.

The 393-feet long roof is supported by ten shallow 'two-hinged' arched ribs. The cantilevered barrel vaults have skylights running the full width of the garage, which together with windows in the side walls and wide entrances, bathes the interior with natural light. Seen from above this gives the impression of a line of dolphins diving in unison. At street level the outward-leaning buttresses appear to effortlessly support the curved roof.

Nicholas Bennett

1953 English Martyrs

Architect: FX Velarde
Location: Wallasey, Merseyside
Type: Place of worship
Listed Grade II*

F.X. Velarde (1897–1960) was largely an ecclesiastical architect who designed predominantly Roman Catholic churches. English Martyrs demonstrates his learned response to the requirements of both the Liturgical Movement and finding an architectural idiom that moved beyond the clash of styles that had marked church design over the previous century. The interiors of his churches express both a sense of transcendence and of 'active participation' in the celebration of the Liturgy. The single unitary internal space, with walls of bare brick, is crossed with a series of thresholds between narthex and nave, and between nave and sanctuary, the latter nearly always expressed with low level wrought iron railings that draw the participant forward rather than form the barrier of popular post Second Vatican Council (1962–65) clerical misconception. The use of plain brick, stone sculpture set in brickwork and elemental historical forms were legacies from his days at Liverpool School of Architecture under Charles Reilly, the use of strong colours from his Catholic piety and art school training. The architectural relationship between transcendence and participation in the liturgical worship makes Velarde's churches exemplars of what contemporary church design should aspire to.

Father Peter Newby

Smithdon High School

Architect: Alison and Peter Smithson
Location: Downs Road, Hunstanton, Norfolk
Type: Education

Alison Smithson was 21, Peter 26, when in 1950 they won a competition for a secondary school in Hunstanton. The symmetrical plan is traditional, its central hall placed between two courtyards, around which classrooms and laboratories are set on the upper floors over ground-floor corridors, offices and cloakrooms.

A welded steel frame, designed on the principle of plastic design that there is no weak point, was inspired by classical forms and Mies van der Rohe. Inside, the unadorned steel ceilings and exposed plumbing are striking. Use of off-the-peg components culminates in a centrally-placed Braithwaite tank.

Alison coined the term New Brutalism to stand for truth to materials and found objects, but it was appropriated by later concrete expressionism, very different to Hunstanton. The direct glazing into the steel frame shattered when the building overheated, solved by introducing wooden sub-frames and black dado panels. The school is now in glorious condition and is much loved.

Elain Harwood

Farnley Hey

Architect: Peter Womersley
Location: Farnley Tyas, West Yorkshire
Type: Housing
Listed Grade II

One of Britain's most celebrated mid-century modern houses, with spectacular views over the Pennines, Farnley Hey was designed by Peter Womersley as a wedding present to his brother. It has been maintained in remarkably original condition. When it was listed in 1998, English Heritage commented: 'In style Farnley Hey suggests the influence of Le Corbusier and Frank Lloyd Wright [...] It typifies the best of the 1950s in its lightness, sense of the picturesque and optimistic stance.'

Farnley Hey is much documented, with attention drawn to the large floor-to-ceiling windows that bring light flooding into the house (as well as giving wonderful far-reaching views). Also much admired is Womersley's exuberant use of materials – from camphorwood and York-stone flags for flooring to the lemon-yellow Formica panels. The defining room of the house – known as The Dancefloor thanks to its polished floors, inbuilt audio system and double-height ceiling – was originally designed for Womersley's energetic parties and even for recording live music. The room also features floor-to-ceiling double-glazed windows.

Albert Hill

1956

Congress House

Architect: David du Rieu Aberdeen
Location: 23–28 Great Russell Street, London
Type: Commercial/offices
Listed Grade II*

Congress House, the headquarters of the Trades Union movement, was above all a symbolic building – symbolic of an alternative form of governance offered by the labour movement. Whereas government buildings were remote, enclosed, monumental corridors of power, Congress House was transparent, engaged with its surroundings, unmonumental, and altogether more open. The design was chosen in 1947 from a competition for which there were 181 entrants, the majority of them traditional, classical or neo-georgian. David Aberdeen's winning design was explicitly 'modern' – he had discovered Le Corbusier's architecture in the 1930s, and applied the lessons he had learnt from the Swiss master here. But Congress House is not strictly Corbusian. A plain curtain wall façade on Great Russell Street is deferential to its neighbours, but the side façade onto Dyott Street erupts with energy – cantilevered balconies fly out of it, a great curved glass stair drum bursts forward at street level, and the upper storeys jump back irregularly. This is a dynamic composition, reminiscent of Russian constructivism of the 1920s, and nothing like it had been seen in Britain before, not even in the work of Tecton.

Having kept all the excitement for the side, the inside is an anticlimax, and Aberdeen's academic training took hold. The interior is arranged around an open court, dominated by a sculpture by Jacob Epstein that was originally backed by an overhanging wall of green Livornese marble (since removed because of corrosion, and replaced by green tiles). As if this monumental set piece were not enough, the plan is rigidly symmetrical around this court – though strangely, the axis of symmetry is not that of the main entrance front, but that of the Dyott Street at the side. But what redeems the interior is the craftsmanship of the joinery and tilework: these are of a quality unobtainable today.

Adrian Forty

Architect: Walter Segal
Location: 22–26 Ovington Square, London
Type: Housing

Memorably described by Pevsner as reminiscent of 'a Morris Traveller parked among grander saloons', this post-war replacement block captures its date completely. To any Londoner over 50, it says: bombsite where restoration was not possible. Planning forced that decision and dictated the high-density replacement. The use of cross walls of load-bearing engineering bricks expressed externally is characteristic of post-war reconstruction (1954–70), although the mock Tudor wooden lattice is unusual. The physical (if not stylistic) relation to its neighbours is sympathetic. Rather than shock, it comes as a pleasant surprise when one chances upon it.

Segal, of course, went on to pioneer self-build housing. Fifteen years later a pastiche would have been more likely here. Does 22–26 Ovington Square deserve protection? Maybe. Should it be valued? Definitely. It was recommended by the Society for listing in the 1990s, but was turned down. Not far away 24–26 Hereford Square (same period, similar setting, by Colin Wilson and Arthur Baker) was listed, then de-listed and will surely be demolished and replaced with a pastiche, eradicating a crucial piece of London history.

Peter Ruback

Hallgate

Architect: Eric Lyons/Span
Location: Blackheath, London
Type: Housing
Listed Grade II

The estates built by the developer Span from the 1950s to the 1980s seem like precious things indeed: a developer, working in another time of massive housing need, which built beautifully designed, affordable, sharply contemporary homes. These are Arcadian estates designed with light social engineering, not so as to cajole you into getting to know your neighbours, but, in that phrase so loved by politicians today, to nudge you.

At Hallgate, a block of 26 flats, this takes a simple form: having your front door opposite your neighbour's, sharing ownership of the freehold and basic facilities such as the gardens, the bin store and the shed for bikes and prams. It's not exactly post-revolutionary USSR. But it's enough. Inside, the flats are designed simply but with an eye to how we were starting to live our lives in late 1950s Britain on the edge of prosperity: space is maximised in the main living room/dining room/kitchen sequence, minimised in the bedrooms and bathrooms; the windows are large, but, with cross ventilation, the rooms keep cool. Materials are affordable and ordinary – concrete, painted brick, weatherboarding – but beautifully detailed. The landscaping is pretty but easy enough for the residents to maintain.

None of this is exceptional. The fact that it *is* speaks volumes about British housing.

Tom Dyckhoff

1959

Bracken House

Architect: Richardson and Houfe
Location: 1 Friday Street, London
Type: Commercial/offices
Listed Grade II*

In 1988, as a Trojan Horse manned by the Thirties Society's commandos, Bracken House forced the gates of the listing system to achieve a rolling rather than fixed end-date, with the rest of post-war architecture following behind. Richardson's elevations, with the quality of their workmanship and materials showed that it was not a washed-out relic but a living and breathing Edwardian among the Teddy Boys.

Equally surprising was what followed. As architects for the original replacement scheme, Michael and Patty Hopkins accepted the *fait accompli* with their Japanese clients, and got permission to replace the central section (built as the printing works) with a structure that sits comfortably in Richardson's embrace while retaining its own integrity. In the process, the conventions of modernism, postmodernism and conservation all shifted in their relationship to each other.

Sadly, two other Richardson masterpieces in the City, the 1914 Moorgate Hall and 1923 Leith House, were lost in the 1980s boom, replaced by lumpy cross-eyed monsters.

Alan Powers

1960

Benton Park School

Architect: Burnet and Tait
Location: Harrogate Road, Rawdon, Leeds
Type: Education

Standing like a proud ocean liner marooned on the crest of a hill, Benton Park School was one of the many pioneering projects built during the great educationalist Sir Alec Clegg's term as Chief Education Officer of the West Riding. Conceived as a factory for learning, complete with a towering 66-feet-high chimney, it brought a shocking dose of modernity to the suburban streets: a bold grouping of concrete-framed slabs with expansive factory glazing, each teaching department separated into its own functional block and connected by elevated walkways.

It is where I went to school, stirring my architectural interests when the crumbling grey concrete frame was painted a dazzling white, revealing this unloved hulk as a finely-tuned composition. The four-storey classroom block, its windows and brick infill panels recessed behind the concrete frame, took on strains of Giuseppe Terragni's projecting white grid at the Casa del Fascio in Como (an allusion that didn't altogether please the headteacher). The full-height glazing of the airy gym block suddenly looked like the workshop wing of the Dessau Bauhaus. Surrounded by playing fields, the complex took on architect Bruce Martin's idea of the perfect school as 'a beautiful shiny thing in the middle of a garden.'

Exploring Benton's rambling concrete complex for the first time, wandering the shifting levels formed by the hillside site, and negotiating the steep slope of the battered plinth for precipitous games of tig, was something of a thrill 20 years ago – and no doubt continues to be today.

Oliver Wainwright

Brasenose College Extensions

Architect: Powell and Moya
Location: Brasenose College, Oxford
Type: Education
Listed Grade II*

This small but influential building for Brasenose College was among the first of a clutch of projects into which Oxford put money and its faith in modern architecture from the late1950s onwards.

The site was that of the bath houses; the solution a series of study bedrooms grouped around two staircases at the wider southern end with ingenious windows to make the best of the interesting views, and a series of single-storey study bedrooms on the narrow-ish land to the north, staggered to create private courtyards. It enhanced the existing buildings, taking no light from them, and produced a harmonious relationship between new and old.

The buildings used a combination of Roach bed and smooth Portland stone for the quoins, with white precast concrete for balustrades. Roofs and cladding were in lead sheet (it was a precursor of many university buildings of distinction by this most talented duo, in Oxford and Cambridge).

It contains staircases of great elegance and geometric complexity, designed by by Jacko Moya, as were the crafted doors to the single storey sets. In my view Moya was a genius.

Richard Burton

1962

Renold Building

Architect: W Arthur Gibbon of Crickshank and Seward
Location: University of Manchester Institute of Science and Technology, Manchester
Type: Education

The Renold Building was designed by W. Arthur Gibbon of Cruickshank and Seward. It was one of a suite of white concrete structures on the UMIST campus in Manchester. It was the first of its type in the UK – an entire building to house lecture theatres and seminar rooms. It is also one of the earliest UK projects to assume a tower and podium configuration after Skidmore, Owings and Merrill's Lever House in New York. The visual separation of the tower was achieved by the use of elegant birds-mouth beams that facilitated the continuous clerestory window at the junction of the two formal elements. Its most striking external feature was the faceted east façade. Also prominent was the stair tower, a perpendicular projection of perilously thin glazing bars. In a nod to Niemeyer and Nervi, Gibbon introduced a curved profile to the rooftop plant room. A fine piece of mainstream British modernism with its roots in the International Style.

Richard Brook

Royal College of Art

Architect: H T Cadbury-Brown with Sir Hugh Casson and Robert Goodden
Location: Kensington Gore, London
Type: Education
Listed Grade II

I have a personal passion for the RCA building, designed by a team including my father, Robert Goodden, who, though trained as an architect, was Professor of Silver and Jewellery, and Pro-Rector of the college. He acted as consultant architect, preparing the brief in consultation with each department and project managing the development. Long after he left, I was also a tutor there.

Its dark austerity contrasts so enormously with the splendid Victoriana of neighbouring Royal Albert Hall and the dazzle of the Consort's memorial opposite, that it stands out like an alien; but this in itself is proof of its power and integrity. It was actually designed to fit in with its neighbours, then covered with black soot. The audacious 'baronial modernism' of the monolith houses a unique workspace purpose-designed for the students of the 1960s, an enormous factory-gallery which has inspired, and continues to generate, the best ideas in the world.

Henrietta Goodden

1964) BT Tower

Architect: Eric Bedford and G R Yeats, Ministry of Public Building and Works
Location: 60 Cleveland St, Marylebone, London
Type: Public building
Listed Grade II

Designed by the architects of the Ministry of Public Building and Works and clearly inspired by the futuristic visions of Gerry Anderson puppet landscapes (*Stingray*, *Thunderbirds*, *et al*) the BT Tower (formerly the Post Office Tower) has been, and for me still is, the icon of the London skyline. With a requirement to have no more than a 10-inch shift in winds up to 95 miles per hour, to keep the microwave dishes in line, the super ridged tube was the only form that would work – but wrapping it all in glass was inspired and always left me, as a child, thinking how lucky those office workers were!

At 634 feet tall it was the tallest building in the UK until it was beaten by the Nat West Tower in 1980, but oh how dull those other behemoth towers were and it is only recently that the London skyline has had tall buildings to rival the silhouette of the BT Tower. Perhaps now that it has been nominated for *100 Buildings*, the rotating restaurant on the 34th floor, amazingly run by Butlins until 1980, could be opened for business once more.

Peter Crawshaw

Cathedral Church of the Holy Spirit

Architect: Edward Maufe
Location: Guildford, Surrey
Type: Place of worship
Listed Grade II*

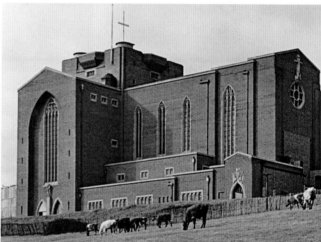

Guildford Cathedral was the only new-build Anglican cathedral on a new site in England started since 1914; Coventry replaced an existing one. It was won in competition by Edward Maufe in 1930, but the war and its aftermath considerably delayed its completion: the cathedral was consecrated in 1961 and the western garths finally completed in 1965. It was built to serve the Diocese of Guildford, newly created in 1927, covering most of Surrey and north east Hampshire. Its brown brick tower, atop Stag Hill outside Guildford, is a landmark from far and near in the best tradition of medieval cathedrals.

What makes Guildford Cathedral special is the interior, which combines Maufe's planning skills and collaboration with designers like Eric Gill, Vernon Hill (statuary), John Hutton (etched glass), Moira Forsyth and Lawrence Lee (stained glass) and his wife Prudence (on carpets and embroidered kneelers). There are recurring themes in all his churches: high roofs contrasting with low passage aisles; and strong contrasts of bare wall and colour in the form of fresco and heraldic design, all embodying the best of Swedish early 20th-century design and Arts and Crafts traditions.

Robert Drake

1966

Our Lady Help of Christians, Tile Cross

Architect: Richard Gilbert Scott
Location: East Meadway, Tile Cross, Birmingham
Type: Place of worship
Listed Grade II

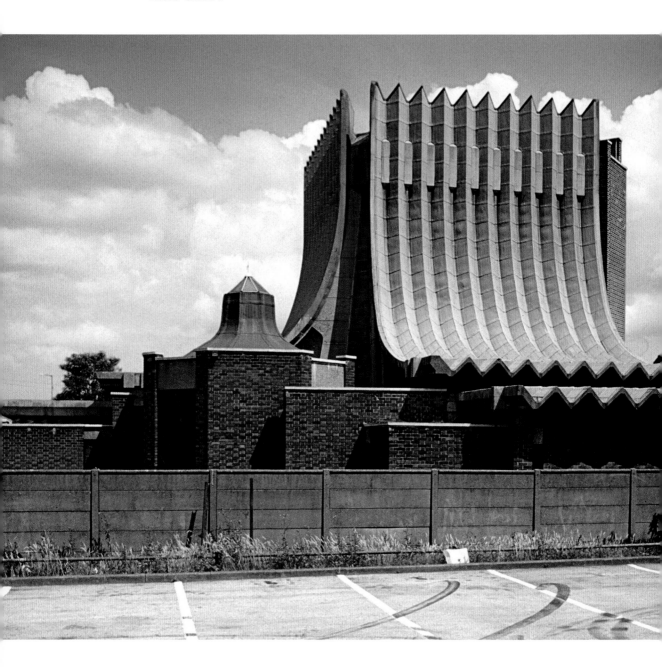

In the 1960s, the Second Vatican Council demanded a radical rethink of the planning of
Roman Catholic churches and resulted in some remarkable and innovative buildings. Two
notable examples are in Birmingham, the work of Richard Gilbert Scott, the architect
son of Sir Giles Gilbert Scott whose practice he continued. The commissions for the
Birmingham churches, however, were inherited from Adrian Gilbert Scott, his uncle. Scott
was given a free hand by the Archbishop, as long as the buildings were cheap. That at Tile
Cross was the architect's favourite of the two (the other is at Sheldon). A subtly polygonal
T-shaped plan allowed a forward altar surrounded by seating. Above this, the roof is partly
formed by extraordinary curved serrated ribbed trusses of reinforced concrete faced
externally in copper – a dramatic, theatrical treatment which suggests both a delight in
expressive, sculptural forms and a desire to continue with the modern Gothic spirit which
the architect's father had done so much to sustain. Inside, the spaces left between the
concrete frame are filled with remarkably good stained glass by John Chrestien. This is one
of the most successful of modern Roman Catholic churches in England.

Gavin Stamp

Southbank Centre

Architect: London County Council Architect's Department
Location: South Bank, London
Type: Entertainment

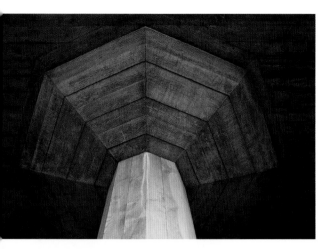

The initial disdain for the Festival Hall was similarly felt for the new Hayward Gallery, Queen Elizabeth Hall and Purcell Room, when the aim of the complex to complement rather than compete with their predecessor was not immediately appreciated.

But the robust details and inherent utility have stood the test of time. The range of remarkable spaces, inside and out, has allowed for a degree of flexibility that none anticipated when they were built. The skateboard Mecca in the extraordinary undercroft, and the roof terraces becoming community gardens all help to add to the 'cultural quarter' – a phrase so frequently overused in regeneration circles – which now fits the wider South Bank.

The current good news is the announcement of a conservation project to address the £24m backlog of repairs to begin in late 2015. These repairs, rather than the grandiloquent and commercially oriented additions of the proposed Festival Wing, currently on hold, should allow the Centre to continue to flourish.

David Heath

Newcastle Civic Centre

Architect: George Kenyon
Location: Haymarket, Newcastle upon Tyne
Type: Public building
Listed Grade II*

With the city on its knees thanks to post-war de-industrialisation, it took infamous city council leader T. Dan Smith, to drag Newcastle kicking and screaming into modernity.

The provincial power base that Smith spearheaded found its home in city architect George Kenyon's civic centre. Fulfilling both administrative and ceremonial roles, this imposing building takes pride of place in the Haymarket area, and offers a sense of spatial drama common to a city of steep inclines and dramatic jump cuts. The Nordic influence is clear, with walls of Norwegian Otta slate offset by the rich walnut and marble of the interiors, and the aged copper finishings of the exterior. A ring of heraldic sea horses circles the building's trident-like tower, a nod to the city's sea-bound heritage, with the impressive 'River God Tyne' sculpture by David Wynne cementing the link further. Other notable contributions include the entranceway by Geoffrey Clarke, and two abstract murals by Victor Pasmore in the cashiers' reception.

T. Dan Smith was jailed for corruption in 1974, a saga immortalised in the BBC drama series 'Our Friends in The North'. However, it's hard to dispute that his plan for Newcastle as a 'cultural capital' is still being played out today.

Richard Smith

Preston Bus Station

Architect: Building Design Partnership
Location: Tithebarn Street, Preston,
Type: Transport
Listed Grade II

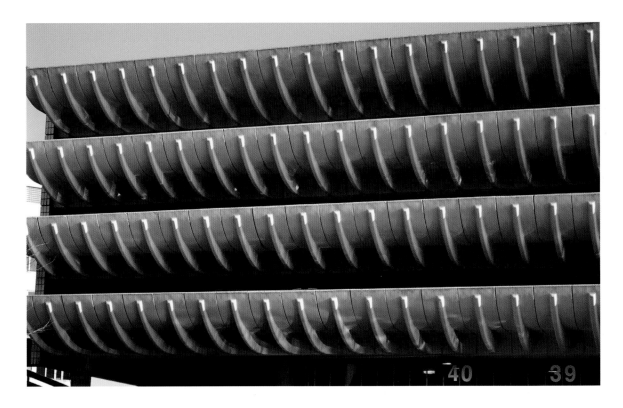

Designed by Keith Ingham and Charles Wilson of Building Design Partnership (now BDP), the Central Car Park and Bus Station in Preston was listed at Grade II in September 2013 after a 15-year campaign. This included a thematic survey of transport buildings and designation selection guide by English Heritage, two attempts to list it by the C20 Society because it was threatened with demolition (2009 and 2012), support from the architectural profession and a grassroots campaign. It also attracted international attention, from the World Monuments Fund and International Council on Monuments and Sites (ICOMOS).

I was the Society's case officer from 2008–12, and researched and wrote the third listing application which re-opened the case and led to its listing. The building's distinctive contribution to the Preston cityscape and the support of both heritage experts and the general public were a driving force throughout my involvement. The positive outcome constitutes a reward for the Society's sustained advocacy of C20 architectural heritage.

Christina Malathouni

Wyndham Court

Architect: Lyons Israel Ellis
Location: Blechynden Terrace, Southampton
Type: Housing

Lyons Israel Ellis, though well known as a finishing school for the famed likes of Stirling, Gowan, Colquhoun *et al*, were the sort of Brutalists that didn't get Yale scholarships, shiny monographs or late careers in pomo. They are found more often designing local authority housing, comprehensive schools and other unsexy things – most of them robust enough to be extant and in good nick. From their Old Vic extension through to the London School of Engineering, they were giants of big, chunky, angular neo-constructivist architecture rife with skylines, cantilevers and complex geometries, all in satisfyingly raw, tactile concrete. As Colquhoun later put it, this was architecture for those who had nothing but contempt for 'the Englishness of English art' and other consolatory narratives.

Their masterpiece, Wyndham Court ought to be as well-known as the Brunswick Centre or the Barbican, and isn't largely because of where it is. It is a monumental, civic housing project on the grandest scale. As a building, it shows more than a hint of rhetoric creeping into LIE's usually astringent aesthetic. Placed just outside Southampton Central Station with a fine view of the docks, its service tower skyline and long, streamlined volumes have more than a hint of the ocean liner about them. Here they arc around a square, with shops on the ground floor, high-density-city centre living for council tenants rather than as an aspirational loft-living lifestyle. A magnificent vote of confidence in a city which has built little of note since, it's also, for me, the building that announces that I'm 'home' far less depressingly than BDP's repugnant WestQuay shopping centre on the other side of the railway line – a massive concrete statement that another city was and still is possible.

Owen Hatherley

Anderton House

Architect: Aldington and Craig
Location: Rigg Side, Goodleigh, Devon
Type: Housing
Listed Grade II*

Ian and May Anderton, family friends of Peter Aldington from Preston, commissioned a retirement home in 1969. Aldington had developed a practice in Buckinghamshire, including a house for himself, that combines concrete block and tiles with old walls and render in historic Haddenham. In Devon, the long house plan set across the hillside similarly reflects local traditions, while the timber frame could be prefabricated under Aldington's scrutiny nearer home.

The complex brief was developed with Aldington's partner John Craig. A pen between the kitchen and living area allowed Mr Anderton to work amid a clutter of papers without being cut off from his meticulously tidy wife.

The Landmark Trust acquired the house after Mrs Anderton's death and restored it with Aldington's help; sourcing appropriate kitchen equipment proved the greatest difficulty. Here is a rare opportunity to stay in a great modern house and savour its high spaces and rich detailing.

Elain Harwood

1972

Trellick Tower

Architect: Ernő Goldfinger
Location: 7 Golborne Rd, London
Type: Housing
Listed Grade II*

Above The separate
lift and service
tower of Trellick
Tower is linked at
every third storey
to the main building.

Above right
Entrance lobby.

Right Inside a flat;
all have access to
a balcony.

Opposite The
31-storey block
of 217 flats.

It's a testament to the Trellick Tower's striking silhouette that at least one west London child grew up believing Father Christmas lived at the top of Ernő Goldfinger's flats. Her parents had no need to reach for a location more exotic than the tower's lofty, sentinel-like control room to articulate their particular version of the story.

Its unique profile means many Londoners – and users of the Westway – feel a sense of attachment to the Trellick Tower that is enjoyed by few other blocks of flats.

It has travelled in the public consciousness from bold symbol of the future to pariah and back again, swapping council tenants for owner-occupiers in the process.

So familiar on the skyline, its form changes thrillingly as one approaches. Inside the surprises are all about colour, from the unexpected stained glass in the lobby to the colour-coding of each floor. The ornamention naturally extends into each flat but I was still startled to find one resident had painted the inside of his balcony vivid orange. I felt like I had been let in on a secret almost as exciting as the one about Father Christmas.

Elizabeth Hopkirk

1973 Roman Catholic Cathedral of SS Peter and Paul

Architect: Percy Thomas Partnership
Location: Pembroke Road, Clifton, Bristol
Type: Place of worship
Listed Grade II*

Described as a 'sermon in concrete' in Pevsner's *Architectural Guide to Bristol* and by Mike Jenner, the architectural historian and critic, as 'one of the great interiors of the last 50 years in Britain', this building has much to commend it.

Designed by the Percy Thomas Partnership and completed in 1973, it was the world's first cathedral designed in response to the Second Vatican Council's emphasis on liturgical requirements. Acccordingly, the altar is brought forward and the congregation is seated around three sides of it. The plan for the building is an irregular hexagon subdivided into varied polygons.

Internally the concrete walls are flooded with light from the funnel-shaped roof lantern light. Externally the building is clad in precast concrete panels faced in granite aggregate and crowned with a tripartite spire. It stands in marked contrast to the surrounding Victorian villas of Pembroke Road.

The structural engineers were Felix Samuely and Partners and the contractors were John Laing. It was built for £600,000 and was called the 'ecclesiastical bargain of the 1970s' as a result.

Bob Hardcastle

1974

Barbican housing

Architect: Chamberlin, Powell and Bon
Location: City of London
Type: Housing/entertainment
Listed Grade II

The Barbican is the greatest work of British planning and architecture of the 20th century, in the great tradition of bloody-minded English Baroque from Vanburgh and Hawksmoor via Nash. In the 1950s the car-free, three-dimensional living city seemed the logical way forward. This is the only really coherent piece that was realised.

There are multiple ground levels – some on the roofs of houses! It is not predicated on buildings simply fronting long streets and squares. Looking up, down, or sideways it is about landscape and building melding into one Piranesian composition and what landscape, what buildings.

The long residential buildings are topped by cheeky white Mediterranean vaults. The idiosyncratic triangular plan towers are craggy with silhouetted balconies – and never bettered. All stand on stonking great rough cylindrical pilotis. A long pedestrian bridge vaults under a building across the lake and into the truly complex arts complex (not completed until 1982). Among other good things this has the best modern theatre space in London: all seats and no aisles.

Chamberlin, Powell and Bon would be way up in the Pantheon for the exquisitely executed Corbusian Golden Lane alone. But it is surpassed by this three-dimensional *tour de force*. Inside and out it is sublime.

Piers Gough

1975 The Willis Building

Architect: Foster Associates
Location: 15 Friars Street, Ipswich
Type: Commercial/offices
Listed Grade I

The former Willis, Faber and Dumas headquarters in Ipswich is one of Foster Associates' earliest schemes. It houses some 1,300 staff in open-plan offices. It had been completed for only 16 years when it was listed Grade I in 1991.

It sits on land virtually surrounded by roads. A grid of concrete columns in the middle support the cantilevered concrete floor and roof slabs, and the perimeter is enclosed with dark glass suspended from their edges. There is a staff restaurant on the top floor, and a swimming pool was originally included in the design.

It is a landmark building in the development of the high tech architectural style. The glass external wall flows around the back edge of the pavement, defining the extent of the building and reflecting its neighbours. The escalators generously move up to each floor in a straight line rather than doubling back. And the roof above the staff restaurant was one of the first to be covered in grass.

David Thomas

The National Theatre is the masterpiece of Denys Lasdun and Partners, and has a good claim to be Britain's finest late-modernist public building. It was commissioned after a protracted, contentious briefing process involving leading English theatre directors including Laurence Olivier and Peter Brook. The fight to get its government funding was tough, and it went on site in 1969 just in time for the strike-ridden 1970s.

By its opening in 1976 its Brutalist style was widely hated, and it was attacked by Prince Charles and others. It is only now emerging from this unfashionability to be recognised as a triumph of sculptural design, humane sublimity, and the highest quality of concrete building-craft. Its free, indoor and outdoor public spaces represent the apogee of the Welfare State's egalitarian generosity, and preside over a bend in the Thames giving views which (at least above the excessive tree-planting) sweep the London cityscape.

Barnabas Calder

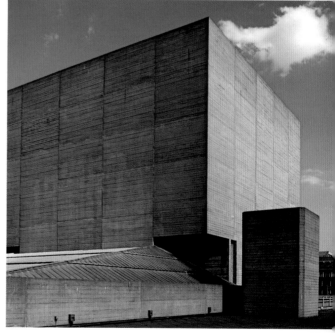

30 Cannon Street

Architect: Whinney, Son and Austen Hall
Location: City of London
Type: Commercial/offices

French bank Credit Lyonnais wanted a prestige headquarters 'discernable from a distance', and must have been delighted by the result. Marooned on one of the City's most prominent traffic islands, close to St Paul's Cathedral, the building purrs 1970s sleek sophistication and pioneering materials.

It was the first building anywhere to be clad in glass fibre reinforced cement (GRC), and the first to incorporate outward leaning windows on a five degree angle. The cream pre-cast panels offer a curved façade of arches with deep angular reveals, a sweeping arcade beautifully offset by bronze tinted glass. Polished black granite bands act as string courses at every floor level, masterfully concealing external drainage to prevent dirt staining the cement.

The top storey is turned on its head like the teeth of a Venus fly trap. But sun trap maybe a better description, as half of the fifth storey is given over to a landscaped deck with GRC flower boxes and seats, and fine views of its majestic neighbour.

Henrietta Billings

1978 Liverpool Anglican Cathedral Church of Christ

Architect: Sir Giles Gilbert Scott
Location: St James's Mount, Liverpool
Type: Place of worship
Listed Grade I

High on St James's Mount, Scott's Gothic, sandstone Cathedral dominates Liverpool.

The 331-feet tower impresses with its height and bulk. The lower part is square, punctuated by the Rankin Porch. The eight-sided upper stage is topped with a lantern crown. The sheer scale of the interior awes: the tower space, the sublime 456-feet nave, and the arched bridge at the west end. The interior is richly decorated: Edward Carter Preston's sculptures, Carl Edwards's stained glass, and fine furniture and woodwork.

Scott's Memorial is at the heart of the nave. He was 22 in 1903 when he became joint-architect with Bodley. After 1907, Scott was the sole architect. The west front was completed in the 1970s: his lifetime's work.

Although the Cathedral houses new works – a recent addition is a Tracey Emin neon – it is surely one of the 20th century's greatest Arts and Crafts buildings. The interior contains many fine artworks and furniture.

Aidan Turner-Bishop

(1979) Milton Keynes Shopping Building

Architect: Stuart Mosscrop and Christopher Woodward,
Milton Keynes Development Corporation
Location: Between Midsummer and Silbury Boulevards, Milton Keynes
Type: Commercial/offices
Listed Grade II

This was the largest shopping centre in the UK and remains the most distinguished.
Milton Keynes is a grid-plan city and the Shopping Building plan picks up the idea: a long
rectangular extrusion.

The Shopping Building puts pedestrians first. Delivery trucks are diverted onto the
roof – you occasionally glimpse them. And shoppers approach all elevations on the level (it
won a pioneering accessibility award). Nowhere do refuse yards, ramps and dead spaces
intrude on one's approach.

Inside, shopping prevails, but retail frontages are kept in line, the lack of visual clutter
so refreshing. It's Miesian, if by that you understand the smallest parts of the architecture
have a clear relationship to the largest elements, on both plan and elevation. It's Miesian
too in carefully detailed joints and finishes, its steel, glass, travertine.

It was listed in 2010 but not before dozens of tiny changes. A larger change was the
indoor planting, once spectacularly lavish. Full-grown trees and giant cacti have given way
to bedding plants. That could – and should – be reversed.

Roland Jeffery

1980 Keble College Extension

Architect: Ahrends, Burton and Koralek
Location: Keble College, Oxford
Type: Education
Listed Grade II*

In the 1970s, with modernism prematurely declared dead, architects had to grope a bit to find a new direction. There were nascent high tech, early postmodernism, and stabs at returning to 'vernacular' architecture. ABK, and especially their Keble building, offered a way that was none of the above. With its satisfyingly solid, castle-like brick walls, and sort-of quadrangle, it refers to the past, but then it brings in curves and slopes of dark glass.

There's a bit of James Stirling in its geometries, and its historic/modern combinations, but realised in a distinctive way. It is a warm, embracing building, with its honeyed brick and half-sunk walkways. It is also a nice way of complementing the overwhelming polychromy of Butterfield's buildings for Keble, while also standing up to them.

All that said, a qualifying note from someone who has lived and worked there: 'The proportions are extremely poky. The materials aren't very nice. My room was either pitch dark or uncomfortably bright/boiling hot depending on the position of the sun.'

Rowan Moore

1981

Hunterian Museum and Art Gallery

Architect: William Whitfield
Location: University Avenue, Glasgow
Type: Higher education/ museum

The dramatic skyline of Whitfield's earlier library is now effectively lost to us, but its neighbour remains a fine example of the architect's interest in forms (in Brutalist clothing) reflecting the peels of his native Northumberland. But what goes on in the largest tower? Fenestration boxed out in contemporary vein, but the individual windows all 19th century or early 20th century in pattern. And a Glasgow Style door in mid-air!

Mid-air, that is to reflect the position and aspect of the door of the (demolished) home of the Mackintoshes, which stood a few yards away. The painstakingly reconstructed interiors are within, along with a recreation of Mackintosh's bedroom at 78 Derngate in the top-floor gallery.

The top-lit picture galleries are quite low-key, to allow the collections to speak for themselves, but are heralded by Paolozzi's monumental cast-aluminium doors. A single oculus lights the sweeping Piranesian staircase. Magical.

Euan McCulloch

1982 Byker Estate

Architect: Ralph Erskine's Arkitektkontor
Location: Byker, Newcastle upon Tyne
Type: Housing
Listed Grade II*

Motorway proposals and partial clearance blighted southern Byker until Erskine was invited to produce outline proposals. He retained churches, pubs and a swimming baths in a rolling redevelopment. Erskine leased an undertaker's shop as an office and drop-in centre, where residents could comment on details. They had no say in the perimeter wall of flats that shields the low-rise elements from the road, metro and north winds, derived from work in arctic Sweden.

Patterned brick walling faces north, but to the south balconies and walkways exploit the benign microclimate. The early low-rise housing has similar roofs and timberwork, and over-scaled downpipes topped with bird boxes. Later areas use oversize bricks and earthier colours. Salvaged Victorian fragments contribute to the careful landscaping.

Listing followed proposals to demolish Bolan Coyne, an isolated block that has now been restored. Byker is the finest public housing of the 1970s and arguably Erskine's greatest achievement.

Elain Harwood

Above View of the Byker Wall looking east.

Right Byker wall looking west. The low-rise housing is just visible amid the trees.

1983 Sainsbury Building, Worcester College

Architect: Richard MacCormac
Location: Worcester College, Oxford
Type: Education

In my third year as an architecture student we were taken to visit to the Sainsbury Building, then under construction at Worcester College, Oxford, with the promise of seeing something quite new. The building was a year away from completion, but it was already evident that the promise would be fulfilled.

When finished, it represented the 'Romantic Pragmaticism' then being promoted by the *Architectural Review*: it was formal and symmetrical in its complex composition and layout, but detailed to suggest the vernacular architecture of the Cotswolds and crafted internally like an Arts and Crafts building. It was set around a lake, and engaged fully with its romantic site. Jonathan Glancey later noted that it had been designed to age gracefully, a novelty at the time.

The project was a first of series of influential buildings for Oxbridge colleges by MacCormac and his subsequent practice, MJP Architects, which have continued to this day.

Timothy Brittain-Catlin

1984 Schlumberger Research Centre

Architect: Michael Hopkins and Partners
Location: Cambridge
Type: Offices

The Schlumberger Research Centre is a stunning high-tech marquee designed by Michael Hopkins and Partners as a research facility for the engineering firm Schlumberger. It consists of two glass office buildings housing offices and laboratories linked by a tented structure, which incorporates both a winter garden as social space and test rigs for the evaluation of drilling techniques and materials. Structurally innovative, it represents the first use in the UK of Teflon-coated glass fibre for building construction.

It is located on high ground outside the city in an area occupied by research facilities, the space around it allowing for expansion and providing a buffer for noise and the potential risk of explosion. As a result, tethered in its field close to the M11, it quickly became an iconic landmark – both to me and to others returning to Cambridge – especially at night, when it seems to float with an ethereal glow.

Clare Price

1985 Burnham Copse Infant School

Architect: Hampshire County Council Architect's Department
Location: New Church Road, Tadley, Hampshire
Type: Education
Demolished

The sweeping, conical roofs of Burnham Copse, decorated in bands of slate, glass and herringbone tiles, were conceived as festive incidents in a bland suburb. Richard Weston suggested that 'Henry Morris would have loved them, for here indeed is a building fit to stand 'side by side with the parish church' as a symbolic centre for the community it serves'. Burnham was one of a remarkable sequence of eclectic, witty and imaginative public buildings designed under the leadership of Hampshire county architect Colin Stansfield Smith (1932–2013).

The variety of nicknames coined by pupils and local residents, including 'tipi', 'circus tent', and 'magic roundabout', suggested that the designers realised their aim of providing an evocative and place-making form. Through its life on the printed page, Burnham Copse will continue to inspire school designers, although it will no longer enchant pupils – it was demolished in August 2010.

Geraint Franklin

1986

Lloyd's Building

Architect: Richard Rogers Partnership, Engineers, Ove Arup and Partners
Location: 1 Lime Street, London
Type: Commercial/offices
Listed Grade I

Res ipsa loquitur: it speaks for itself, and doesn't really need a supporting statement.
I had just graduated from university, and had started my first job in the City as the Lloyd's building neared completion. It was a building like no other and it stood out in so many ways. In the early 1980s there were very few tall buildings in London, and it (literally) stood out on the London skyline (like Wren's spires must have after the rebuilding of London following the Great Fire). But it also stood out as being radically different from any other London building. No other had its services – plumbing, electricals, staircases and lifts on the outside, leaving an uncluttered space inside. The inherent flexibility in the design has meant that it has survived as a commercially useful building remarkably well. The C20 Society sought a Grade I listing in 2008 and this was granted in 2011, just 30 years after work on the site began.

As the listing entry says, the building 'firmly retains the splendour of its awe-inspiring futuristic design, 25 years [at the time of listing in 2011] after it opened.' Doesn't it just?

Nicholas Aleksander

Broadgate

Architect: Peter Foggo
Location: City of London
Type: Commercial/offices

The initial four phases of Broadgate, the largest and defining commercial development of its time in the City, were created between the developers appointed by British Rail and the multi-disciplinary design team of which I was a member. The heart of the complex is a unique central pedestrian square and circle with a colonnade clad in travertine marble about which the offices are arranged, which is a popular focal point for activities including, until recently, winter ice skating. It is intersected by pedestrian routes accessing the lower ground Liverpool St Station and the local surroundings segregated from vehicular and bus movements.

The office buildings of composite steel frame and concrete construction remain as leading examples of efficiency and the large floorplates created are internally enhanced by daylight from dramatic glazed atria. The unified façades of the offices at lower levels utilise granite screens to reduce glare and solar gain whilst the upper storeys are set back to improve daylight within the square, all enhanced at ground level by sculpture and high quality surface material.

Tony Taylor

1988 Isle of Dogs Pumping Station

Architect: John Outram
Location: Stewart Street, Isle of Dogs, London
Type: Public building

I have lots of favourite 20th century buildings, but I have chosen this one as it is such fun. The style is postmodern, which is much maligned, but to me represents the attitude of the 1980s: a decade when flashy was fashionable.

It is tucked away in the Docklands in London and built at a time when this area was on the verge of being transformed by towering developments such as Canary Wharf. This, in contrast, is a small building, but it makes a big statement: a 'Temple of Storms', full of Egyptian and mystical symbolism. If the Victorians could build beautifully decorative pumping stations, why shouldn't the tradition be taken up again a century later?

I am in distinguished company, by the way, in liking this building: the Prince of Wales called it 'witty and amusing'!

Clare Price

Postmodernism
Timothy Brittain-Catlin

In his book *New British Architecture* of 1989, the critic Jonathan Glancey wrote that the 'architect had descended from Parnassus to the market place'. That was no doubt an observation prompted by the unfamiliar sight of different styles jostling together for attention where previously – so it had seemed to modernism's critics – there had only been one, embodied in a dreary, state-promoted monolith, grey in colour, faced with concrete, proposed by a property developer and yet promoted by the local council, and possibly occupying a site across a ring road where once there had been a noble Victorian church or pretty Georgian terrace.

That was only rarely true of architecture by the late 1970s, but the critics were circling: David Watkin in Cambridge; Christopher Booker, in a polemical 1979 film for the BBC called *City of Towers*; the historian and journalist Gavin Stamp; and eventually the Prince of Wales, whose public opposition to Ahrends, Burton and Koralek's competition-winning scheme for an extension to the National Gallery was largely responsible for its cancellation. And architects were already responding with buildings that were multicoloured and multi-shaped. Glancey's book included the rich, jewel-like walls and interiors of John Outram's New House, at Wadham in Sussex (1986), its six different cladding materials including the architect's own tutti-frutti 'Blitzcrete'; Julyan Wickham's City wine bars, epitomised by the brash brass-and-mirrors of Corney and Barrow (1983); Terry Farrell's Henley Regatta headquarters at Henley, with its ultramarine Venetian window and acroteria (1985); and Campbell Zogolovitch Wilkinson Gough's Aztec West industrial estate outside Bristol, a monumental Egyptian tomb of a building designed for mundane purposes and completed in 1988. The new colours

Above The dramatic escalators at Foster's Canary Wharf station.

and shapes and the free references to historical decorative styles constituted 'postmodernism' in architecture. Farrell's temple-like Clifton Nurseries building, which went up in Covent Garden between 1980 and 1981, and is now demolished, drew at the time more attention than its tiny size might have suggested; and yet in retrospect it really did mark the turning of a corner. As Glancey remarked in his opening sentence: 'After more than 20 years of not-so-splendid isolation, British architects have begun to form a fresh relationship with the public in the 1980s'.

In fact by that period the crisis in British architecture, if it had ever existed, was over: a series of projects large and small, from the Byker Wall

Above CZWG's Circle apartment buildings in Bermondsey.

the Victorian enthusiast Mark Girouard had admired in the *Review*. If Keble was 'Gothic', then Worcester was 'Classical', a picturesque British compromise. It seemed that some British architects born in the decade before the Second World War had grown up not just as modernists, but modernists full of humanity and warmth. Romantic Pragmatism could be seen on a modest but persistent scale in the schools designed by the Architect's Department of Hampshire County Council under Colin Stansfield Smith and, to this day, in the work of Edward Cullinan: a characteristic work is his Fountains Abbey Visitor Centre, completed in 1992 for the National Trust, with its sweeping roof, dry-stone walling and rustic timber detailing with prominent pegs.

The 'isolation' that Glancey referred to was the dearth in the 1970s of major commissions in Britain for first-rate architects; but in the new decade, and ever since, those who then seemed the most experimental found themselves employed and treasured. An exhibition at the Royal Academy in 1986 canonised them: 'New Architecture: Foster, Rogers, Stirling.' Rogers's Lloyd's Building, in Lime Street in London for a notably conservative client, was completed that year; equally impressive was Foster's Hong Kong and Shanghai Bank headquarters in Hong Kong, then the most expensive building per square foot in the world; his Sainsbury Centre at the University of East Anglia had already made his popular reputation in the same way that the Pompidou Centre had done for Rogers. Whatever the commercial and exclusive nature of the brief and client for the two buildings, these were structures designed for public involvement and discussion, through the enticing and complex models and drawings exhibited at the Academy as much as in reality. In common with the architecture of Nicholas Grimshaw, the works of Rogers and Foster had about them not only the character of that universally admired figure, the Victorian engineer, but also the obsessive aesthetic control and craft detailing of Pugin. Finally and after a long interval an architecture had emerged that had broad public appeal, and it was one that could be traced to earlier and distinctly British episodes in architectural

(under construction since 1969) to the Greater London Council's much praised Odham's Walk estate, had shown that late modern architects were developing a deep sensitivity to their craft and were overcoming the dogmatic and puritanical aspects of modernism that were so disliked, not to mention the earlier faith in production-line building technologies. For some, the word 'craft' was the key. The *Architectural Review* under Peter Davey championed the 'Romantic Pragmatists': architects who saw themselves in the Puginian tradition of designing buildings as a way of enriching society, and who, like Pugin himself, aimed to do it through high-quality workmanship and rich, innovative detailing, rather than through formal games and slick, smooth surfaces (or for that matter, historical styles). Richard MacCormac's Sainsbury Building at Worcester College, Oxford (1983), was the first swallow. It was indeed romantic: symmetrical; set around a lake with oriel windows; and bounded by a free stone wall; and yet it seemed a natural development from ABK's recent new wing at Keble College nearby, with its sinuous glazed walkways and its almost castellated exterior, a building which history. What can also now be said with certainty is that with the emergence and development of its high-profile, high-tech architects, the influence of British architecture could be felt in Europe and the Americas for the first time since the Arts and Crafts Movement.

Stirling, the third architect at the Royal Academy show, appears to be a different matter altogether; just as Farrell's divorce from Grimshaw had turned him from sleek modernist to pioneer postmodernist, so Stirling's detachment from Gowan had had a similar effect. In common with Rogers he had built almost nothing in Britain during the 1970s: it was the Stuttgart Neue Staatsgalerie (1984) that had signalled his return to a British audience, and with that all semblance of his technological, orthogonal past vanished. No. 1, Poultry, in the City of London, was his posthumous swansong: not completed until 1997, four years after his death, its stripy, curved body, its swaggering, provocative curved forms, and the round clock tower at its apex with its curious wings, seem to refer back to the first anti-modern backlash, or possibly even to the Gotham City of the 1989 film *Batman* by the British designer Anton Furst. The British Library, finally completed in 1998, was likewise the eventual result of a very slow process of design and construction, and also seemed at the time of its opening to be something of a throwback – this time, to some 25 years beforehand when its architect Colin St John Wilson had first conceived it as a homage to the Nordic modernists he admired.

The exhibitionist architectural styles of the 1980s continued into the next decade only in the form of a few very large projects already underway; the theme of the coming period was one of greater intellectual development. The most lasting new ideas may well turn out to be those of the architecture of the sustainable environment: a branch of Sainsbury's in Greenwich, 1999, ironically now under threat of demolition, was the first building to make an impact in this way; in the current decade, the debate over low-energy, carbon-conscious and sustainable design eventually became the principal theme in contemporary architecture. Alongside that, the formal composition of façades and plans has made a comeback, invariably aided by computer software.

A series of Maggie's Centres, commissioned by the theoretician and historian Charles Jencks, has offered well-known architects the opportunity to pursue their ideas on a very small scale, and here and elsewhere a willingness to engage with the immediate landscape and its landmarks or traditional forms became important. Caruso St John are in some ways the model for this new type of architect; both are theorists and teachers, whilst their best-known buildings – The New Art Gallery Walsall (2000) and the Nottingham Contemporary (2009) – make reference to local building and craft traditions. Comparable is Níall McLaughlin, whose housing at Stratford on the 2012 Olympic site is decorated with panels that resemble ancient Greek reliefs; his Bishop Edward King Chapel, Cuddesdon (2013), has a combination of intellectual themes and complex geometry, but also radiates a friendliness and warmth.

Finally: if architecture was at an ebb because of low public investment at the start of the 1980s, it has benefitted for the last 20 years from a stream of public funding, in particular from the Heritage Lottery Fund, which first received applications for capital projects in 1994. It was this fund which supported, among many other significant buildings, the Hepworth, David Chipperfield's gallery in Wakefield; the remodelling of the Shakespeare Memorial Theatre in Stratford-upon-Avon by Bennetts; and Wilkinson Eyre's Gateshead Millennium Bridge. A new enthusiasm for railway architecture has provided us with the fine stations of the Jubilee Line Extension, commissioned by Roland Paoletti; Grimshaw's former Eurostar terminal at Waterloo; and the magnificent restoration and remodelling of St Pancras. Thus the period thus ends with a show of public confidence in design which seemed unthinkable in 1980.

1989

Italian Centre, Merchant City

Architect: Page & Park
Location: Ingram Street, Glasgow
Type: Commercial/offices

The Italian Centre in Ingram Street in Glasgow, designed by the local firm of Page and Park, is not a single, discrete work of architecture but a subtle, sympathetic integration of new and old. That is part of its significance. It marked a change, coming as it did after a long period that saw the neglect and demolition of many of Glasgow's historic buildings and the destruction of much of its urban fabric by motorways.

The Italian Centre is a development of shops, cafés and offices around a new courtyard which marked a return to civilised urbanism and a recognition of the importance of continuity, by retaining several 19th-century classical stone façades facing the surround streets. The new fabric – unassertive and vaguely postmodern but inventive and humane – was enhanced by new sculpture by Jack Sloan while the Italian theme was proclaimed by figures and friezes on the exterior by the modern neo-classical sculptor Alexander Stoddart. The success of the Italian Centre confirmed a change of direction in Glasgow which led to the regeneration of the historic Merchant City.

Gavin Stamp

Vauxhall Cross

Architect: Terry Farrell
Location: 865 Albert Embankment, London
Type: Offices

Terry Farrell's Vauxhall Cross, widely known as the headquarters of MI6, has been blown up twice – in the James Bond movies *The World Is Not Enough* (1999) and *Skyfall* (2012). I imagine a few hardline modernists cheered as the place went up. The building, one of a trio of big London projects which marked Farrell's conversion to postmodernism, has been controversial from the time of its completion more than 20 years ago. Denys Lasdun, who had an office facing it across the Thames, particularly loathed it – just as Nikolaus Pevsner loathed Wallis Gilbert's Hoover Building, now revered as a Deco icon. Tastes change, and my prediction is that Farrell's building will eventually be recognised as one of the more distinguished products of the brief flowering of British postmodernism in the 1980s. Its eclecticism offends some but, as Charles Jencks remarked, 'who said Postmodernism is pure?' How superior Vauxhall Cross is to most of the subsequent development along the river: forget stylistic issues, this is a building which responds to and enhances its setting.

Ken Powell

1a Kingdon Avenue, Prickwillow

Architect: EllisMiller Architects
Location: Prickwillow, Ely, Cambridgeshire
Type: Housing

The Fens resemble California only in their wide skies. Jonathan Ellis-Miller, raised in Norfolk, nevertheless chose to build a steel-framed house after completing his training at the University of Liverpool. He was working for John Winter, whose influence is seen in the three-bay steel frame, one bay left open as a car port, with white chosen to contrast with the black fens. The central bay houses the living room and kitchen, and the other the study and bedroom/bathrooms. The front elevation is glazed to maximise the distant view of Ely Cathedral, while the others combine glass with profiled steel, which also lines the ceilings and internal partitions. The main and kitchen door are adjacent, so Ellis-Miller could enter one door and his muddy Dalmatian, Hector, the other.

The tiny house is simply and coolly elegant, reviving enthusiasm for cheap, architect-designed houses and leading to further commissions. It can now be rented for holidays.

Elain Harwood

1992 Fountains Abbey Visitor Centre

Architect: Edward Cullinan
Location: Ripon, North Yorkshire
Type: Museum/heritage

The Fountains Abbey Visitor Centre is a delightful building arranged around a courtyard, which enhances the experience of coming to this historic site. It is an exemplar project, which set the standard against which all future facilities of this type would be measured.

A careful blend of traditional materials and the use of grassy embankments against the perimeter help to root the building in the landscape. There are steeply pitched slate roofs juxtaposed with softly curved lead roofs, dry-stone external walls and bespoke cedar-framed glazed screens and windows, all of which complement the rural setting.

There are trademark elements of Cullinan's quirky individuality expressed on the sloping ceilings of the interior, and in the lighting arrays mounted on their coloured battens. This helps to give the building a playfulness that the general public seem to have warmed to.

This is an uncompromisingly modern building which respects its heritage context, and yet it embraces visitors as soon as they walk into the courtyard, framing a view of the Abbey tower in the distance. For me it simply still has the 'wow' factor, which has stood the test of time.

Paul Barnfather

Tate St Ives

Architect: Evans and Shalev
Location: St Ives, Cornwall
Type: Art gallery

St Ives was the centre of English artistic creativity in the 20th century. Tate Gallery's acquisition of Hepworth's sculpture garden in 1976 was followed by this major gallery overlooking Porthmeor Beach, housing the Tate's collections and bringing international exhibitions to Cornwall.

Eldred Evans's early modernist schemes remained unrealised, or have been demolished, but she reasserted her career in 1984 with the postmodern Truro law courts, and won a competition for St Ives in 1989. This too is monumental: a blowsy contrast to the subtle works within and stung by the tang of the sea. The view is framed as an artwork that almost usurps the man-made works exhibited in a series of studio spaces. The white entrance drum was inspired by the columnated gallery at the National Museum of Wales, where Evans had curated a show of her father's work. The gallery's popularity has prompted a series of proposed extensions.

Elain Harwood

Glyndebourne Opera House

Architect: Michael and Patty Hopkins
Location: Glynde, East Sussex
Type: Entertainment

I nominate Michael and Patty Hopkins' Glyndebourne Opera House. The chance to build a large-scale purpose-designed theatre in the country in the late 20th century has been rare indeed. What I love about this building is the way that it creates a sense of occasion and excitement without pomposity.

The building posed a challenge in its close proximity to Sir George Christie's family home, a red brick neo-elizabethan building set in magnificent country house gardens, the traditional setting for those champagne picnics in the long interval of the opera.

The Hopkins' response was to build in a manner that was absolutely functional and modern, blatantly so in the structure of the flytower. At the same time there's a sense of sympathy and poetry in their selection of traditional materials: handmade bricks, silver grey lead roofing, reclaimed pitch pine that gives the auditorium its almost magic glow.

I agree with Marcus Binney when he calls the Glyndebourne Opera House 'not just a triumph but a great masterpiece'.

Fiona MacCarthy

Opposite The new Glyndebourne, designed to blend into its surroundings. It was the first purpose-built opera house constructed in the UK since John Christie built the original at Glyndebourne.

Left The foyer of Glndebourne opera house has a tented roof structure.

Below The horseshoe-shaped auditorium, built to seat 1,200, is lit with small lamps to give a soft, warm glow.

(1995) Judge Institute

Architect: John Outram
Location: Trumpington Street, Cambridge
Type: Education

The University of Cambridge's Judge Business School occupies the old Addenbrooke's Hospital. Mostly designed by Matthew Digby Wyatt in the 1860s, the building fell vacant in 1984 and was subsequently listed. In 1990, John Outram won the commission to refurbish and extend it.

Outram added three new structures behind the retained 1860s building (with a new cornice and portico). The Ark contains academics' offices, while the Castle houses lecture theatres and plant. The Gallery, a 79-feet-tall space defined by giant columns and criss-crossed by stair bridges, links everything together.

Outram was critical of much recent university architecture, thinking that it hid the intellectual ambition of its users. His design is distinguished by a rich, allusive vocabulary which makes liberal references to architectural history and theory. Colour is a key feature, inspired by ancient Greek and Victorian precedent. This is Outram's biggest work, and one of the best examples of postmodernism in Britain. It offers a playful contrast with the typical sobriety of business-school architecture.

Alistair Fair

Architect: Richard Murphy
Location: Edinburgh
Type: Healthcare

Richard Murphy designed our first of many cancer caring centres named after my late wife Maggie, who had a hand in the initial layout. The interior, focused on the kitchen table – an informal space around which various activities pivot – is a light and colour-filled area, the antithesis of the antiseptic anonymity of the large hospital machine. Most spaces are multi-functional throughout the week as they shift from private consultations to group meetings, raising funds to guided research on the web.

An old stable block was converted by Murphy into a time-building that asserts its mixed ages and compound functions. Highly coloured metal, glass block and wood are threaded through the previous heavy greywacke. The contradictory materials enhance each other; the layered space resolves complexities that have to work on top of each other. The result is cheerful without being cloying, rather like an early house by Norman Shaw or Frank Lloyd Wright. In the1890s, had they bothered with 'isms', they might have called it 'inglenookism,' a quality of most Maggie Centres. Extended several times, this time-building epitomises the subtle art of rehab.

Charles Jencks

No. 1 Poultry is London's very own Egyptian temple. In rather better nick than the Roman Temple of Mithras nearby, it occupies one of the City's most prominent corners. Prince Charles, whose objection to a Mies skyscraper laid its foundations, nonetheless dismissed it as resembling a 1930s wireless set.

But to me its monumental elevations, beak-like climaxes and Tutankhamun stripes shout Valley of the Kings. Epically scaled, it stretches for two blocks without monotony, its exuberant roofline rewarding extended gazing.

At street level a thick curtain has been pulled back allowing passers-by to glimpse the holy of holies – or Bucklersbury Passage, as it is known. Stepping inside, one expects to find an eternal flame burning. Instead railings invite one to pause and contemplate the void.

And now the building's sense of humour is revealed. Look up to discover an oculus lifted high on walls of incongruous colour, material and rectilinearity.

In the heart of this temple to commerce is a shrine that appears to be made from fragments of social housing.

Elizabeth Hopkirk

British Library

Architect: Colin St John Wilson
Location: Euston Road, London
Type: Public building

Colin St John Wilson's work on the British Library began in 1962, in partnership with Leslie Martin for a site in Bloomsbury, and ended with the completion of the building (in truncated form) at St Pancras in 1997 and its official opening by the Queen the following year. The frustrating course of the project, with many false starts, had led Peter Hall to name it as a 'Great Planning Disaster', and yet the finished library precisely conveys Wilson's ambitions for a grand national building in the spirit of the 'other tradition' of modern architecture, by which he mainly meant the legacy of Alvar Aalto.

This is a humane building, executed under the exacting eye of its architect down to the Aaltoesque details of its door handles and with the integration of artworks by friends. The central glass box containing The King's Library was a late change, following the supplanting by computer terminals of a traditional catalogue hall.

Timothy Brittain-Catlin

1999 Sainsbury's Eco-store

Architect: Chetwood Associates
Location: Greenwich, London
Type: Commercial/offices

Sainsbury's pioneering eco-designed supermarket fits neatly into the two dominant meta-narratives of the late 20th century: shopping as destination experience, and the move to sustainable building. Designed by Chetwood Associates after much research, the Eco-store was opened by that other 1990s icon, TV chef Jamie Oliver. It was the first store to be awarded the BREEAM excellent rating: by installing CHP, and using daylight rather than artificial lighting, it consumed 50% less energy than a conventional supermarket.

Its distinctive zoomorphic shape highlights landscaping by the Woodland Trust and minimises light pollution. Pedestrian, cycling and public transport access are integrated and even electric charging points provided. It won the 2000 RIBA Sustainability Award, was short listed for the Stirling Prize and customers loved it. Despite being called at the time 'the high point of supermarket design in the 20th century' the Eco-store is now threatened with demolition. Will this example of sustainable development survive?

Frank Krikhaar

2000

The New Art Gallery Walsall

Architect: Caruso St John
Location: Gallery Square, Walsall
Type: Art gallery

In the flurry of public projects stimulated by the National Lottery, the New Art Gallery Walsall stood out. Where other buildings turned to the future or the past, to bulbous futurism or to heritage, the gallery is rooted in the present, in its time and place. It takes cues unsnobbishly from 1960s towers even as it carries hints of Florentine palaces. It is dignified but also unexpected, in its combinations of concrete and terracotta, and of mass and lightness. It is physical, not abstract, in its materials and light. It is a proud civic monument that also makes sense of the ragged edges of its site. Unlike some other Lottery projects it also has some content, with a reasonably good art collection at its core. And it was the breakthrough project for some outstanding young architects, selected through competition. Again, this doesn't happen often enough.

Rowan Moore

2001) Eden Project

Architect: Nicholas Grimshaw
Location: Bodelva, St Blazey, Cornwall
Type: Entertainment

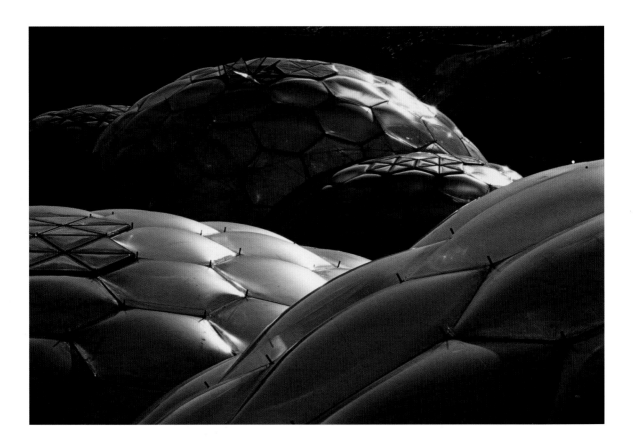

'The Eden Project's iconic biomes, the world's largest conservatories, are a symbol of a living theatre of plants and people, of regeneration and of a pioneering forum for the exploration of possible futures' wrote Tim Smit, originator of the project. His eco-vision was realised by Nicholas Grimshaw and engineers Anthony Hunt and Associates with Arup as the services engineers. Since 2001 it has attracted over 13 million visitors to view the thousands of plant species housed in the domes.

The basis for the geodesic biome domes came from the work of the American engineer J. Baldwin, a pupil of Buckminster Fuller, who developed a system of 'pillow domes'. These were constructed from tubular steel with hexagonal translucent cladding panels made from TPE thermoplastic film and erected by MERO for McAlpine, the main contractors. As part of Eden's policy of providing environmental education, the Core has recently been built to meet their requirements for exhibitions and teaching.

Bob Hardcastle

2002 Gateshead Millennium Bridge

Architect: Wilkinson Eyre
Location: South Shore Road, Gateshead
Type: Transport

The Millennium Bridge is the world's first and only tilting bridge, designed by Wilkinson Eyre Architects and engineered by Gifford. A grand demonstration of innovative precision engineering, it opens like a huge eye to allow ships to pass underneath and takes its place at the end of a line of distinguished bridges across the River Tyne.

It was spectacularly transported upriver and lowered into place by one of the world's largest floating cranes, Asian Hercules II, with 36,000 people lining the banks of the Tyne to watch it tilt for the first time. 413 feet in length and 164 feet high in its normal state, the bridge is made up of two steel arches – one deck comprises of the pedestrian and cycle path (an almost-horizontal curve, hanging from a series of suspension cables) whilst the other supporting deck forms an arc over the river. It acts as an important link between Newcastle and Gateshead and has significantly contributed to the rejuvenation of the Quayside area.

Karen Topping

2003 Selfridges

Architect: Future Systems
Location: The Bullring, Birmingham
Type: Retail

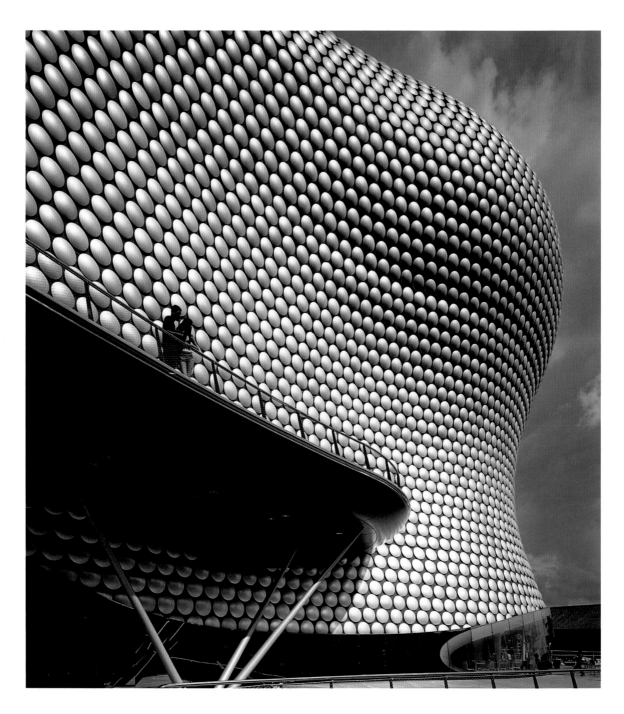

Birmingham's architecture is eclectic and most Brummies accept the randomness of the buildings around them as the norm. Selfridges, bulging out of the city's Bullring shopping centre, appears a bit like a fly's compound eye thanks to the thousands of aluminium discs on its façade. It celebrates the constant ambition of Brummies to reinvent their city; an optmistic symbol of Birmingham's recent regeneration.

The department store replaced a multi-storey car park of an uninspiring quality. I remember how, below the car park, there was a decaying warren of pedestrian subways and shop units, which briefly in the 1980s formed a proto-Chinatown made up of several businesses: one was a resturant run by my grandparents. In its place, I'm happy to see that Future Systems have created a memorable building that looks certain to outlast the timid and mundane shopping centre around it.

Wilson Yau

2004 — Scottish Parliament Building

Architect: EMBT/RMJM
Location: Holyrood, Edinburgh
Type: Public building

Few buildings divide opinion as profoundly as Scotland's new parliament. A hard fought architectural competition brought together Enric Miralles of Barcelona-based EMBT with what was then one of the world's largest architectural practices, RMJM.

The landscape moves in, around and over the structure, deftly making the transition between Edinburgh's Old Town and the Queen's Park behind. With the restored Queensberry House at its heart, the parliament combines three buildings of quite distinct character, from all angles, full of variety and intrigue. The lack of orthogonals imbues every room with interest. The two main gathering spaces, the Parliament Chamber and the Garden Lobby, revel in Enric Miralles's shape-making.

Despite Miralles's untimely death in 2000, a sometimes difficult marriage of practices undoubtedly delivered the icon to which he aspired. With all its richness, the building will, in time, be recognised as one of the great works of European architecture of this, or indeed any other century.

Neil Baxter

Vauxhall Bus Station

Architect: Arup Associates
Location: Vauxhall Cross, London
Type: Transport

When I became MP in 1989, Vauxhall Cross was an anonymous windswept wasteland between the railway and the river.

Magically, from between the cranes and the concrete mixers, this amazing, stylish construction, Arup's Vauxhall Bus Station, arose. A gleaming elevated ribbon of stainless steel, the canopy undulates above the buses to soar away into two enormous cantilevers, quickly nicknamed 'the Ski Jump', and now a famous identifying landmark for Vauxhall.

The elegant form follows the hugely successful function, where at ground level the bus platform allows passengers to change safely and quickly under cover. This is civic space at its best, valued and used by everyone, whether office cleaners taking night buses to the city, revellers returning from the club scene, or local resident Lords taking a bus to Westminster.

Lambeth Council, so pleased to welcome its construction a decade ago, now wish, against howls of protest, to demolish it and replace it with a row of shops.

Kate Hoey

2006

Brunswick Centre

Architect: Patrick Hodgkinson (initially with Leslie Martin)
Refurbishment: Levitt Bernstein Associates
Location: Brunswick Square, Bloomsbury, London
Type: Housing/retail
Listed Grade II

Plans for the Brunswick Centre began as a 40-storey office block in 1959. As reconfigured from 1961 onwards it pioneered low-rise, high-density, mixed-use development. After many iterations, the built scheme comprised 560 flats, shops, restaurants, the Renoir cinema, a health centre and small offices. Camden acquired the lease of the flats, which remain predominantly social and sheltered housing, with some private leaseholds.

Flats are well laid out and full of light; each has a living room with a glazed wall opening onto a balcony, and a kitchen with breakfast bar. The reinforced concrete A-frames inside the two residential blocks create dramatic cathedral-like views: my daily pleasure.

By the1990s, it was run down and the concrete badly weathered. Allied London redeveloped it to plans by Levitt Bernstein and Hodgkinson, closing the north end with a new supermarket and painting the exterior, as originally intended. Completed in 2006, it now has the fashionable shops, cafés, and Saturday market Hodgkinson always wanted.

Susannah Charlton

East Beach Café

Architect: Thomas Heatherwick
Location: Littlehampton
Type: Commercial/offices

In 2005, after buying a house in Littlehampton, I noticed that the small kiosk across the green had planning permission for a large and rather unattractive café. I decided to buy the kiosk and build something of architectural merit that would enhance the promenade.

I knew of the emerging talent of Thomas Heatherwick and readily agreed when we met by chance and he asked to design it. The studio responded beautifully to the brief, creating a form that fitted into the surrounding beach and framed views of the sea. My daughter Sophie and I opened a restaurant to reflect the quality of the building.

It has won a total of 27 awards for design (and the food!) and its huge success has shown that good architecture is also good business. I love the building now as I loved it when I saw it emerging from the foundations; there is nothing about its design or function I would change.

Jane Wood

2008

Accordia Housing

Architect: Fielden Clegg Bradley (masterplan and lead architects) with Maccreanor Lavington and Alison Brooks Architects
Location: Brooklands Avenue, Cambridge
Type: Housing (166 flats and 212 houses)

The site was once the landscaped grounds of Brooklands House, now the local office of English Heritage, which were subsequently developed with temporary government buildings during the Second World War. A re-development brief by Cambridge City Council evolved into a masterplan that gained planning permission in 2003. Construction started immediately and was essentially completed in 2008.

The design used a pale brick similar to the traditional Cambridge Gault brick. The buildings achieved a high density in clusters of 65 with courtyards and roof terraces instead of gardens. Between them, full use is made of the mature landscape for communal open space. Described as 'High-density housing at its very best', the scheme has won a dozen awards including the 2008 RIBA Stirling Prize, the first for a housing development.

In 2014, following a detailed appraisal, the boundary of the Brooklands Avenue Conservation Area was extended to include the Accordia development. This is perhaps a unique example of a scheme going from 'new' to 'heritage' in less than a decade.

Chezel Bird and Eddie Booth

2009

Artists' Studios, Aberystwyth Arts Centre

Architect: Thomas Heatherwick
Location: Aberystwyth, Wales
Type: Arts/education

Sixteen artists' studios, wrapped in BacoFoil, gently shimmering amid foliage. Welcome to Aber. This is Thomas Heatherwick's winning competition entry for start-up 'creative units' at Aberystwyth Arts Centre. At once futurist and home-made, Heatherwick's woodside pavilions are a kind of fulfilment of Peter Cook's 1972 vision of 'a Quietly Technologised Folk-Suburbia'.

Heatherwick's low-cost cladding system was based on sheets of steel the thickness of a drink can, specially crinkled in a crinkling mangle, wrapped around timber battens, and stiffened with spray-on insulation foam backing. Will it all stand up to the ravages of time, a coastal climate and art students? Does that matter? An image has been realised, and that is what counts.

The final word goes to Mary Lloyd Jones, the celebrated Welsh painter and one of the first occupants: 'One of the reasons for applying for a residency was because of the light in the studio – so beautiful'.

Geraint Franklin

Architect: Elizabeth Scott, refurbished by Bennetts Associates
Location: Waterside, Stratford-upon-Avon, Warwickshire
Type: Entertainment
Listed Grade II*

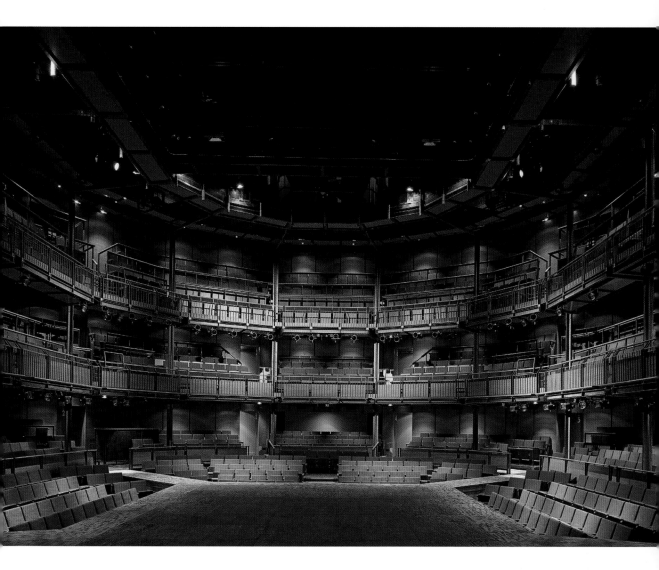

Elizabeth Scott's 1932 Royal Shakespeare Theatre is significant as an exemplar of modernism and as the first notable building to be designed by a female architect. Praised by some for the close attention to detail that was unusual in a monumental modern structure, its use of high-quality natural materials and the simple elegance of the decorative characteristics of the building, the theatre was derided by others for its industrial idiom and lack of reference to the heritage of the locality.

The 2010 redevelopment by Bennetts Associates brought the theatre up-to-date with today's preferences by working pragmatically within the historic fabric of the building. A complete demolition of the original auditorium space has made way for the construction of a thrust stage which provides a more intimate theatre experience, while elsewhere the most successful elements of Scott's original design have been carefully restored. As it stands today, the building is well loved and its many historical layers work in harmony with each other within the riverside context.

Teresa Pinto

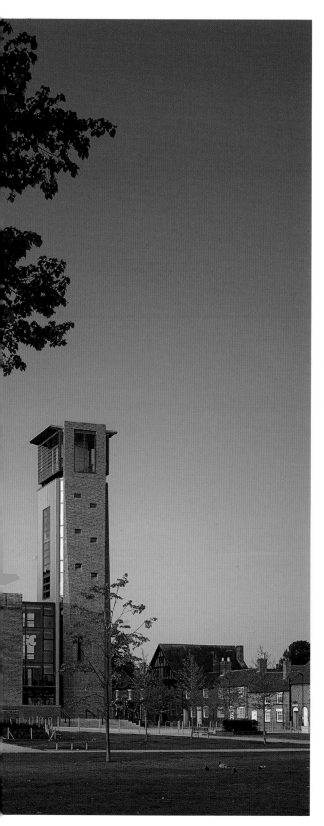

Above The new theatre retained the Art Deco interiors of the existing foyer.

Left The transformation of Elizabeth Scott's original Royal Shakespeare theatre held onto key historical elements of the building and incorporated new architecture, including a glazed colonade and the tower with a 108-foot-high viewing gallery.

2011

Hepworth Gallery

Architect: David Chipperfield
Location: Gallery Walk, Wakefield, Yorkshire
Type: Museum

I liked the Hepworth Gallery from the outset, and was able to walk round inside it with Simon Wallis (its director) well before any art had arrived. And now I like it more every time I visit. It always had the feeling of a stage, or a raft, lifted up above its surroundings, almost as if it were moored there for a while but might move on in time. This sense of suspension has a slightly destabilising effect which I like. It throws you a bit off-kilter, and enlivens the circulation of the building. I very much like its circularity, the varied but even plays of light, the balance of bigger and smaller spaces, and the contrast between the lower entrance level – which seems quite functional – and the upper galleries, which are working well for the art, and in ways which are surprisingly flexible. Its location is nicely unexpected, and the barges and boats haphazardly gathered by the weir add to the other-worldly sense that the whole edifice might somehow float away.

Penelope Curtis

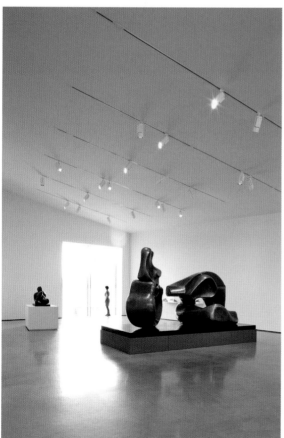

2012

Aquatics Centre

Architect: Zaha Hadid
Location: Stratford, London
Type: Sport

The Aquatics Centre is an astonishing legacy of the 2012 Olympics. Designed by Zaha Hadid in 2004, before London won the bid, it went through a number of transformations before its present incarnation as the most spectacular neighbourhood pool in the UK. Dominated by its wave-like roof, the original design was revised to cut costs and then modified again in order to accommodate 18,000 spectators during the Olympic games, when it acquired two wings.

In March 2014 it reopened, with the wings replaced by two stunning glass walls. The facilities now include a 50m competition pool, the diving pool immortalised by Tom Daley and a 50m training pool. The 50m pool is 10-feet-deep, and the diving pool has platform boards at heights of 3m, 5m, 7.5m and 10m, all made out of curved concrete.

Swimming in the pool is a sensational experience, getting into the building less so as the apparently grand entrance is not the way in and access appears to be underground. Apart from this minor defect, it stands as one of the few venues in Olympic history that has genuinely become a local community asset.

Paul Lincoln

2013 Bishop Edward King Chapel

Architect: Nìaill McLaughlin
Location: Cuddesdon, Oxfordshire
Type: Place of worship

The Bishop King Edward Chapel is an exquisitely crafted building that follows a great tradition in light and geometry. Built for Ripon Theological College and a small resident community of nuns, the elliptical chapel's exterior wall is of Clipsham stone set in dogtooth style. Inside, a delicate ship-like structure of latticed woodwork draws the eye to dappled light from the surrounding trees.

Niaill McLaughlin melds client needs and contemporary technology in a seamless way giving a strong sense of identity and pride to its community and place. He is a rare breed, a research practitioner, and the chapel the result of a rigorous and lyrical research process.

Flora Samuel

Further reading

Gerald Adler, *Robert Maguire & Keith Murray*, London, RIBA, 2012

John Allan, *Berthold Lubetkin, architecture and the tradition of progress*, London, Black Dog, 2014

Marcus Binney, *In Search of the Perfect House: 500 of the best buildings in Britain and Ireland*, London, Weidenfeld and Nicholson, 2007

Edmund Bird and Fiona Price, *Lambeth Architecture 1914-1939*, London, Lambeth Archives, 2013.

Timothy Brittain-Catlin, *Leonard Manasseh and Partners*, London, RIBA, 2010

Timothy Brittain-Catlin, *Bleak Houses: Disappointment and failure in architecture*, Cambridge, MIT Press, 2014

Lucy Bullivant, *British Built, UK architecture's rising generation*, New York, Princeton, 2005

Nicholas Bullock, *Building the Post-War World, Modern architecture and reconstruction in Britain*, London, Routledge, 2002

Catherine Burke, *A Life in Education and Architecture: Mary Beaumont Medd*, Farnham, Ashgate, 2013

Rutter Carroll, *Ryder and Yates,* London, RIBA, 2009

Tony Chapman, *The Stirling Prize: ten years of architecture and innovation*, London, Merrell, 2006

Susannah Charlton, Elain Harwood & Alan Powers, ed., *Twentieth Century Architecture 8: British Modern*, London, C20 Society, 2008

Celia Mary Clark & Robert Cook, *The Tricorn: The Life and Death of a Sixties Icon*, Portsmouth, Tricon Books, 2010

Alan Clawley, *John Madin*, London, RIBA, 2011

Catherine Croft, *Concrete Architecture*, London, Laurence King, 2005

Elizabeth Cumming and Wendy Kaplan, *The Arts and Crafts Movement*, London, Thames and Hudson, 1991

Penelope Curtis, *Patio and Pavilion: the place of sculpture in modern architecture*, London, Ridinghouse, 2007.

Trevor Dannatt, *Modern Architecture in Britain*, London, Batsford, 1959

Gillian Darley and David McKie, *Ian Nairn: Words in place*, Nottingham, Five Leaves, 2013

Elizabeth Darling, *Re-Forming Britain, narratives of modernity before reconstruction*, London, Routledge, 2007

Elizabeth Darling, *Wells Coates*, London, RIBA, 2012

Peter Davey, *Arts and Crafts Architecture*, London, Phaidon, 1990

Edward Denison, *McMorran & Whitby,* London, RIBA, 2009

Arthur Edwards, *The Design of Suburbia*, London, Pembridge, 1981

Robert Elwall, *Building a Better Tomorrow*, Chichester, Wiley Academy, 1999

Adrian Forty, *Words and Buildings: a vocabulary of modern architecture*, London, Thames and Hudson, 2000

Adrian Forty, *Concrete and Culture: a material history*, London, Reaktion Books, 2012.

John R. Gold, *The Experience of Modernism*, London, Routledge, 1997

John R. Gold, *The Practice of Modernism*, London, Routledge, 2007

Henrietta Goodden, *The Lion and the Unicorn, Symbolic architecture for the Festival of Britain 1951*, London, Unicorn Press, 2011

Jeremy Gould, *Plymouth: Vision of a modern city*, Swindon, English Heritage, 2011.

John Grindrod, *Concretopia: A Journey around the Rebuilding of Postwar Britain*, London, Old Street Publishing, 2013

Samantha Hardingham, *England, a guide to recent architecture*, London, Ellipsis, 1995

Elain Harwood & Alan Powers, ed., *Twentieth Century Architecture 5: Festival of Britain*, London, C20 Society, 2001

Elain Harwood & Alan Powers, ed., *Twentieth Century Architecture 6: The Sixties*, London, C20 Society, 2002

Elain Harwood, *England: a guide to post-war listed buildings*, London, Batsford, 2003

Elain Harwood & Alan Powers, ed., *Twentieth Century Architecture 9: Housing the Twentieth Century*, London, C20 Society, 2008

Elain Harwood & Alan Powers, *Tayler and Green*, London, Prince of Wales Institute of Architecture, 1998

Elain Harwood, *Chamberlin, Powell & Bon,* London, RIBA, 2011

Elain Harwood & Alan Powers, ed., *Twentieth Century Architecture 10: The Seventies*, London, C20 Society, 2012

Elain Harwood, Alan Powers & Otto Saumarez-Smith, ed., *Twentieth Century Architecture 11: Oxford and Cambridge*, London, C20 Society, 2014

Elain Harwood, *Space, Hope and Brutalism, English architecture 1945-75*, London, Yale, 2014

Owen Hatherley, *Militant Modernism*, London, Zero Books, 2009

Owen Hatherley, *A New Kind of Bleak*, London, Verso, 2012

David Heathcote, *Barbican: Penthouse over the City*, Chichester, John Wiley & Sons, 2004

Bevis Hillier, *Art Deco of the 20s and 30s*, London, Studio Vista, 1968

Lesley Jackson, *Contemporary*, London, Phaidon, 1994

Lesley Jackson, *The Sixties*, London, Phaidon, 1998

Charles Jencks and Edwin Heathcote, *The Architecture of Hope: Maggie's cancer caring centres*, London, Frances Lincoln, 2010

Simon Jenkins, 'The Anger of Firestone', pp 1-2, *Thirties Society Journal 1*, London, 1981

Adrian Jones & Chris Matthews, *Towns in Britain: Jones the Planner*, London, Five Leaves Publications, 2014

Sutherland Lyall, *The State of British Architecture*, London, Architectural Press, 1980

Fiona MacCarthy, *British Design since 1880: a visual history*, London, Lund Humphries, 1982

Fiona MacCarthy, *Eric Gill*, London, Faber and Faber, 1989, 2011

Duncan Macmillan, *Scotland's Shrine*, Farnham, Lund Humphries, 2014

Robert Maxwell, *New British Architecture*, London, Thames and Hudson, 1972

Noel Moffett, *The Best of British Architecture*, London E & FN Spon, 1993

Rowan Moore, *The New Art Gallery Walsall*, London, Batsford, 2003

Rowan Moore, *Why We Build*, London, Picador, 2012

Kenneth Powell, 'Post-Modern Triumphs in London' *Architectural Design* special issue, 1991

Kenneth Powell, *Powell & Moya*, London, RIBA, 2009

Kenneth Powell, *Ahrends, Burton and Koralek*, London, RIBA, 2012

Alan Powers, *The Twentieth Century House in Britain*, London, Aurum Press, 2004

Alan Powers, *Modern: the Modern Movement in Britain*, London, Merrell, 2005

Alan Powers, *Britain, modern architectures in history*, London, Reaktion, 2007

Alan Powers, *Aldington, Craig & Collinge*, London, RIBA, 2009

Andrew Saint, *Towards a Social Architecture, the role of school building in post-war England*, London, Yale, 1987

Flora Samuel & Inge Linder-Gaillard, *Sacred Concrete: The Churches of Le Corbusier*, Berlin, Birkhauser Verlag, 2013

Dennis Sharp & Sally Rendel, *Connell, Ward and Lucas: A Modernist Architecture in England*, London, Frances Lincoln, 2008

Joan Skinner, 'The Firestone Factory 1928-1980', pp 11-22, *Twentieth Century Architecture 1: Industrial Architecture*, London, C20 Society, 1994

Gavin Stamp, ed., 'The Thirties', *Architectural Design* special issue, November 1979

Gavin Stamp, ed., *Twentieth Century Architecture 2: The Modern House Revisited*, London, C20 Society, 1996

Gavin Stamp, *The Memorial to the Missing of the Somme*, London, Profile Books, 2006

Gavin Stamp, 'Neo-Tudor and its Enemies' in *Architectural History*, vol.49, 2006

Gavin Stamp, *Anti-Ugly: Excursions in English Architecture and Design*, London, Aurum Press, 2013

Anthony Symondson, *Stephen Dykes Bower*, London, RIBA, 2011

Obituary of Brian Anthony, *The Times*, 5 April 2014

Sarah Whittingham, *Wills Memorial Building*, Bristol, University of Bristol, 2003

Index

Picture credits

Pavilion Books Group and C20 Society are committed to respecting the intellectual property rights of others. We have therefore taken all reasonable efforts to ensure that the reproduction of all contents on these pages is done with the full consent of the copyright owners. If you are aware of unintentional omissions, please contact the company directly so that any necessary corrections may be made for future editions.

Front Cover and p.60: © Dean Thorpe www.aspexdesign.co.uk
© Alan Ainsworth Photography: p101, p.131, p.151, p.158 (right).
© John Allan: p.63.
© David Anderson: p.98.
© Zoë Anspach: p.78.
© Architectural Press Archive/RIBA Library Photographs Collection: p.57, p.64, p.65, p.92.
© Avanti Architects, photo Nick Kane: p.58–59.
© Avanti Architects, courtesy of John Allan: p.66, (top) p.66 (bottom).
© Dave Beaven: p.116.
© Hélène Binet: p.172, p.173.
© Elisabeth Blanchet: p.76 (top), p.76 (bottom), p.77.
© C20 Society p.10 (bottom), p.53 (top), p.150.
© Steve Cadman: p.109 (right top), p.135.
© Barnabas Calder/ National Theatre: p.129 (top).
Courtesy of Camden Local Studies Archive: p.182.
© Martin Charles/ RIBA Library Photographs Collection: p.159, p.161.
© The Cinema Theatre Association: p.50.
© Peter Cook: p.188, p.189, p.191, p.192, p.193.
© Tim Crocker: p.6, p.95.
© Catherine Croft: p.7, p.8.
© James O. Davies/ English Heritage: p.72, p.82 (top), p.87, p.89, p.90, p.91, p.97 (left and right), p.103, p.105, p.117, p.118, p.119, p.126, p.133, p.139.
© Dell & Wainwright/RIBA Library Photographs Collection: p.68.
© Sarah J Duncan: p.2, p.11, p.23 (left and right), p.36, p.55, p.62 (left and right), p.85 (top), p.102, p.107, p.112, p.113, (left top and, left bottom and right), p.120 (top left), p.121, p.128, p.129 (bottom), p.130, p.152, p.164 (left and right), p.165 (left and right),p.176, p.177, p.178, p.181, p.184, p.194, p.195 (top), p.195 (bottom left and bottom right), p.196–7.
© John East: p.2, p.32, p.49, p.55, p.56 (bottom), p.85 (bottom), p.93, p.96, p.122, p.132, p.145, p.146, p.148, p.149 (left and right), p.155, p.186.
© John East: p21, p.32, p.49, p.56 (bottom), p.85 (bottom), p.93, p.96, p.122, p.132, p.145, p.146, p.147, p.149 (left and right), p.155, p.186.
© Eden Project: p.174.
© EllisMiller Architects: p.156.
© English Heritage: p.51, p.56 (top), p.127, p.134.
© English Heritage, Images of England: p.37.
© English Heritage, courtesy of Templewood Primary School: p82 (bottom), p.83.
© Jeremy Estop, MJP Architects Ltd: p.142.
© Alistair Fair: p.162 (left and right).
© Ben Foster/ Eden Project: p.175.
© Richard Glover, courtesy of Chetwoods Architects: p.170 (top), p.171 (bottom).
© Jeremy Gould: p.79 (left and right).
© Damian Grady/English Heritage: p.88.
© Greenwich Heritage Centre p.22.
© Ian Grundy: p.30.
© Paul Grundy: p.166 (left and right), p.167, p.168–9.

Courtesy of Guildford Cathedral Archives: p.108, p.109 (left), p.109 (right bottom).
© Aaron Guy: p.114, p.115 (top), p.115 (bottom left).
© Alec Hamilton: p.26.
© Elain Harwood: p.42 (top), p.48, p.52, p.53 (bottom), p.86, p.94, p.115 (bottom right), p.138, p.140, p.141, p.158 (left).
By permission of Clare Hastings: p.31 (bottom).
© Louis Hellman/*Architect's Journal*: p.9, p.10 (top).
© Paul Hinkin, Black Architecture: p.170 (bottom), p.171 (top).
© Elizabeth Hopkirk: p.120 (top right and bottom).
© Impington Village College, courtesy of Amy Wormald: p.69.
© Dr David J Jefferies: p.39.
© Nicholas Kane: p.199 (top left).
© Sylvia Le Comber: p.38.
© Richard Learoyd: p.157.
©London Metropolitan Archives, City of London: p.75.
© London Transport: p.28.
© Lawrence Mackman: p.147.
© Adrian Neil Maltby: p.143.
© John Maltby/RIBA Library Photographs Archives: p.67.
© Manchester Libraries, Information and Archives, Manchester City Council: p.104.
© Rachael Marshall: p.73.
© Euan McCulloch: p.136, p.137.
© Niall McLaughlin: p.198, p.199 (top right), p.199 (bottom).
© David and Mary Medd, owned by Institute of Education: p.144.
© Constantin Meyer: p.185.
© James Morris: p.187.
© Richard Murphy Architects: p.163 (left and right).
© Alison Needler: p.40.
© Philip Paris: p.74.
Courtesy of P. Powell p.123, p.124, p.125.
© Alan Powers: p.61, 84.
© Antonia Reeve: p.44, p.45.
© RIBA Library Photographs Collection: p.99.
© Royal College of Art Archives: p.106.
Courtesy of the RSC, copyright unknown p.190 (top and bottom).
© SAVE/ Marcus Binney: p.70.
© Rob Scott p.41 (right).
© Scottish Parliamentary Corporate Body – 2012. Licensed under the Open Scottish Parliament Licence v1.0: p.180.
© Cela Selley p.71 (left and right).
© Gavin Stamp: p.24, p.25, p.27, 31 (top), p.46 (top) Firestone Factory taken in 1980, p.54, p.110, p.111, p.154 (left and right). Courtesy of Gavin Stamp: p.29, p.35 (left) The Cenotaph and body of the Unknown Warrior passing in 1920, p.35 (right) Observing the Great Silence at the temporary Cenotaph, Whitehall 1919, p.100.
© Jim Stephenson: p.80, p.81(top), p.81 (bottom).
© Stuart Tappin: p.183 (top and bottom).
© The Trustees of 78 Derngate, Northampton: p.33.
© Trustees of the British Museum: p.20.
©University of Bristol Library, Special Collections: p.41 (left).
© Morley von Sternberg: p.160 (top), p.160 (bottom).
© Wallis, Gilbert & Partners: p.46 (bottom), p.47.
© Jennie Walmsley: p.34.
© Welwyn Garden City Heritage Trust Archive: p.42 (bottom left and right), p.43.
© Wilson Yau: p.179.

Acknowledgements

C20 Society would like to thank all those who nominated buildings or supplied photos for this project, including those whose entries we have not been able to include here. You can see more photographs of many of these buildings on our online gallery www.c20society. org.uk/100-buildings, and some alternative nominations are posted on our Facebook page. Thanks also to James O. Davies, Sarah J. Duncan, Nigel Wilkins of English Heritage Archives, RIBA, Professor Christine Whitehead and Professor Peter Williams for their help and advice.

Nicholas Aleksander Solicitor with an amateur enthusiast's interest in the built environment

John Allan Consultant architect to Avanti Architects and a visiting professor of Sheffield University

Paul Barnfather Architect and enthusiastic amateur photographer

Neil Baxter Secretary and treasurer of the Royal Incorporation of Architects in Scotland

Nicholas Bennett Former MP and government minister and later Chief Executive of the Association of Consulting Engineers

Henrietta Billings Senior conservation adviser at the C20 Society

Marcus Binney Founder of SAVE Britain's Heritage and the Thirties Society, and architectural correspondent of *The Times*

Chezel Bird Director of the Conservation Studio and a former historic areas adviser at English Heritage

Edmund Bird Heritage advisor to the Greater London Authority and Transport for London

Elisabeth Blanchet Freelance photographer who opened 17 Meliot Road as the Prefab Museum in 2014

Eddie Booth Director of the Conservation Studio and a former historic areas adviser at English Heritage

Timothy Brittain-Catlin Architect, historian, senior lecturer at the University of Kent and vice-chairman of the C20 Society

Richard Brook Architect and senior lecturer at Manchester University

Richard Burton Architect and co-founder of Ahrends, Burton and Koralek after working for Powell and Moya at Brasenose College

Barnabas Calder Teaches at Liverpool University, and writes on British brutalism and Denys Lasdun

Susannah Charlton Consultant and manager of the C20 Society's website

Peter Crawshaw Co-founder and director of Lovereading.co.uk

Catherine Croft Director of the C20 Society

Penelope Curtis Director of Tate Britain

Gillian Darley Historian, journalist and president of the C20 Society

Elizabeth Darling Reader in architectural history at Oxford Brookes University

Trustees of 78 Derngate

Robert Drake Honorary secretary and trustee of the C20 Society

Tom Dyckhoff Historian, writer and broadcaster, and senior research associate at the Bartlett School of Architecture

Alistair Fair A chancellor's fellow at Edinburgh College of Art

Adrian Forty Professor of architectural history at the Bartlett School of Architecture

Geraint Franklin Architectural investigator with English Heritage

Henrietta Goodden Design writer and former senior tutor at the Royal College of Art

Piers Gough Architect and professor of architecture at the Royal Academy Schools

Jeremy Gould Architect and writer, and former head of architecture at Plymouth University

Alec Hamilton DPhil student in Architectural History, Kellogg College, Oxford

Bob Hardcastle Retired architect

Elain Harwood Historian with English Heritage and trustee of the C20 Society

Owen Hatherley Freelance writer, journalist and blogger

David Heath Architect with English Heritage 1987–2007 and chairman of the Society for the Protection of Ancient Buildings

Albert Hill Founder of The Modern House estate agency in 2004, and previously design editor at Wallpaper

Rosemary Hill Writer, historian and independent scholar

Bevis Hillier Art historian and journalist; first chairman of the Thirties Society

Kate Hoey MP for Lambeth Vauxhall

Nicholas Holmes Completing a PhD on E. Vincent Harris at Sheffield University

Elizabeth Hopkirk Reporter for Building Design specialising in international news

Roland Jeffery Director of Historic Chapels Trust.

Charles Jencks Architectural theorist and critic, landscape architect and co-founder of Maggie's Cancer Caring Centres with his late wife Maggie Keswick.

Frank Krikhaar Global corporate responsibility manager at Aegis Media and volunteer at C20 Society

Paul Lincoln Director of policy and communications at the Landscape Institute

Fiona MacCarthy Biographer and historian, and former president of the C20 Society

Euan McCulloch Enthusiast

Ian McInnes Surveyor and chair of the C20 Society's casework committee.

Duncan Macmillan Art critic at *The Scotsman*, freelance lecturer and author

Christina Malathouni Architect and historian, and a lecturer at Liverpool University

Christine Hui Lan Manley Architect and historian who recently completed a PhD on housing design in Harlow

Charlotte de Mille Art historian based at the Courtauld Gallery

Rowan Moore Architecture critic

Fr Peter Newby Parish priest of St Mary Moorfields and formerly Catholic chaplain at Oxford University

Teresa Pinto MA Student and volunteer C20 Society caseworker

Alan Powers Freelance architectural historian, trustee and former chairman of the C20 Society

Claire Price Conservation adviser at the C20 Society

David Rock Architect and graphic designer, and former president of the RIBA

Peter Ruback Chair of the C20 Society and formerly deputy director for council housing finance and affordable housing in the Department of Communities and Local Government

Andrew Saint Head of the Survey of London

Flora Samuel Architect and head of the School of Architecture at Sheffield University.

Cela Selley C20 Society's volunteer co-ordinator and its former administrator

Richard Smith North Eastern Film Maker, currently helping develop a housing series for Vice Media

Gavin Stamp Freelance architectural historian

Tony Taylor Engineer who worked on Broadgate with architect Peter Foggo at Arup Associates

David Thomas Retired architect and volunteer at C20 Society

Karen Topping Artist and north-east regional representative of C20 Society with her husband John.

Aidan Turner-Bishop Retired librarian and north-west regional representative of C20 Society

Oliver Wainwright Architecture and design critic for *The Guardian*

Richard Waite News editor for the Architects' Journal.

Sarah Whittingham Historian specialising in architecture and gardens, notably in Bristol and an expert on ferneries.

Sarah Wittekind Housing Officer with a keen amateur interest in C20th architecture

Jane Wood Owner of East Beach Cafe

Amy Wormald Development and Engagement Manager, Impington Village College

Wilson Yau Former architectural student, now living and working in London